"LAUNCH PAD: friendly and access..experts that will help any writer put their best marketing foot forward. You can flip to a specific chapter to find answers to your burning questions or read it cover to cover for an in-depth overview of useful marketing tips and tricks." ~James River Writers

"The ideal resource for any stage of the publishing process, Launch Pad offers insider tips to help authors navigate the marketing and publicity piece of this complex industry. The end result? A step-by-step strategy to help writers of all levels identify and reach their target readers in today's crowded market." ~Julie Cantrell, New York Times and USA Today bestselling author of Perennials

"Launch Pad is an essential book for those writers/authors who want to not only jumpstart their marketing strategy but launch it into best-selling status. With each chapter setting out an important cornerstone for success, you'll be grateful you picked up this valuable resource to refer back to time and time again. A must have in your marketing tool box." ~ Meg Nocero, award-winning author of The Magical Guide to Bliss, Sparkle & Shine and Butterfly Awakens.

"An essential addition to every writer's bookshelf! The strategies compiled in Launch Pad provide an indispensable guide to marketing and promoting with authenticity and substance. Communication is the buzzword to connecting, engaging and building relationships with readers. This book has it all." ~ Patricia Sands, award-winning author of The Secrets We Hide

Launch Pad: The Countdown to Marketing Your Book

Mary Helen Sheriff
Grace Sammon

Launch Pad: The Countdown to Marketing Your Book

Copyright © 2023 by Mary Helen Sheriff and Grace Sammon

All rights reserved.

Published by Red Penguin Books

Bellerose Village, New York

Library of Congress Control Number:

ISBN

Print 978-1-63777-378-9 / 978-1-63777-376-5

Digital 978-1-63777-377-2

No part of this book may be reproduced in any form or by any electronic or mechanical means, including information storage and retrieval systems, without written permission from the author, except for the use of brief quotations in a book review.

The views and opinions expressed are those of the individual authors and do not necessarily reflect the views and opinions of the book sponsors.

Contents

Foreword	vii
Introduction	xi
1. THE BRAND CALLED YOU! PERSONAL & PROFESSIONAL BRANDING FOR AUTHORS Lisa Montanaro	1
2. CREATING YOUR PUBLIC RELATIONS PLAN Joelle Polisky	25
3. WHAT IS SHAMELESS SELF-PROMOTION? Erika Lance	45
4. ON BEING A GOOD LITERARY CITIZEN Claire Fullerton	61
5. WHAT EVERY AUTHOR SHOULD KNOW ABOUT BUILDING THEIR WEBSITE Natalie Obando	75
6. SOCIAL MEDIA Meredith R. Stoddard	89
7. LEVERAGE THE POWER OF FACEBOOK Sharvette Mitchell	113
8. CREATING EFFECTIVE AUTHOR NEWSLETTERS Rebecca Rosenberg	135
9. AN EVENTFUL DAY Jade Dee & Wilnona Marie	149
10. HOW TO GET MORE BOOK REVIEWS Annie McDonnell	163
11. BOOK CLUBS Linda Ulleseit	179

12. HOW MUCH SHOULD AN AUTHOR GIVE
     AWAY?   193
     Renea Winchester

13. SUCCESSFUL BOOK PROMOTION
     STRATEGIES   209
     Mary Helen Sheriff

14. THE MAGIC OF SHOWING UP: NETWORKING,
     COLLABORATION, AND COMMUNITY   227
     Katharine Herndon

Afterword   241
Next Steps   247

Foreword

I have worked with thousands of writers over the years, and I have found that they often approach the concept of marketing with dread. They are concerned that they aren't good at it, or that if they pursue it, they will be a sellout, or that regardless of what they try, it won't be effective. In helping writers reach their readers, I want to encourage you to focus on the most critical factor: your mindset.

In this book, you will be reading a lot of specific strategies and tactics for how to get the word out about your book, grow your following, and encourage book sales. Some of these ideas will resonate with you, some won't. The key difference between you effectively using them or not is your mindset.

Instead of worrying about "building an audience" or "growing a following" or "establishing my platform," I want to encourage you to focus on one person. Because each and every person who reads your book, each person you reach through an email newsletter, a book reading, a social media post, or any other capacity—will not feel part of an "audience." They will be having a personal experience between themselves and your writing, or themselves and you. If you want to understand how you can best grow your platform and share your writing, it is at this level—thinking of the individual reader—that will tell you everything you need to know.

Instead of concerning yourself with the algorithms and trends of a certain social media channel or marketing tactic, consider the experiences you want to create for yourself and others. Don't look for the magic button, the shortcut, where you mimic "best practices" that stopped working well years ago. Instead, consider the specific ways that the themes you write about connect to a reader's identity or experience they want to have. How can you make that connection frequently? Through what channels? What questions could you ask, stories could you share, or updates would get them to lean in and become interested? How can you tap into the things that resonate with why they read books like yours?

Too many authors approach marketing with a fear that they must be utilizing the latest trends and feel overwhelmed in the process. I find the opposite creates the most effective way to reach readers: get radical clarity of your purpose. Why do you write? What themes drive you? How would sharing this affect your ideal readers? Where do they tend to show up? What language resonates with them? What would get them to take notice and engage, even if in a small way? How is this process fueled by connection, not promotion?

Besides these questions leading to a more authentic and fulfilling process for sharing your work, they also become the basis of word-of-mouth marketing. What is that? It's what all writers dream of: readers recommending you and your writing to others.

Instead of throwing spaghetti at the wall, trying many different tactics, and always being frustrated that "nothing works," focus your attention, then measure progress every week. I would prefer that you double down on just one or two marketing tactics to share your work than try to juggle an endless to-do list of tasks. It's easy to become distracted by marketing because the internet is likely feeding you endless ideas and stories from others of "X worked for this bestselling author!" Or "Y no longer works, don't waste your time."

When you focus on creating meaningful experiences for yourself and your ideal readers, you rid yourself of the endless search for the right trend, to understand an algorithm, or find that secret magic button. Instead, you judge success based on who you connect with and how meaningful that connection feels. You measure it with moments that matter and the feeling that your work resonates with readers.

As you do the work recommended in this book, regularly assess what you are learning in the process. Don't worry about numbers as much as the experiences and conversations you have with others. Every quarter, take a step back and consider how you need to adjust.

Sharing your writing is about connecting why you write to those who want to experience the world in a certain way. Books are a gateway to so many things. Consider the manner by which you share in the same regard. And if you are unsure of where to begin, just ask, "How can I make one reader smile today?"

Dan Blank is the founder of WeGrowMedia, where he helps writers develop their author platforms, connect with readers, and launch their books. He is the author of the book *Be the Gateway: A Practical Guide to Sharing Your Creative Work and Engaging an Audience*. He has worked with thousands of writers and amazing organizations that support creative people such as Penguin Random House, Sesame Workshop, Hachette Book Group, Workman Publishing, J. Walter Thompson, Abrams Books, Writers House, *The Kenyon Review*, *Writer's Digest*, *Library Journal*, and many others.

Website: https://WeGrowMedia.com

Introduction

Your book tells a story.

Your book is a work of art.

Your book reflects your mind, heart, and soul.

And . . . your book is a product. Book marketing is the process of turning potential readers into customers who buy your book. This anthology is your guide to building awareness of your book, selling your book, and gaining a loyal fan base of readers.

When I signed my first book contract in 2019, I knew the two decades I had spent teaching had not prepared me for the challenge of marketing a book, so I committed to learning how to market and by doing so giving my debut novel *Boop and Eve's Road Trip* every chance to thrive. I read books, listened to podcasts, took classes, designed a marketing plan, hired a publicist . . . all of the things. I vowed to have no regrets and to leave no stone unturned.

While I was able to cobble together resources, the lack of books on the topic surprised me. The few that I did find were often out-of-date, and since book marketing is ever-evolving, old advice might actually be terrible advice. Yikes! Therefore, when Grace Sammon approached me about putting together this anthology, the idea of gathering together the brilliance of seventeen successful authors and book marketers to help authors navigate the book marketing world excited me.

This book is practical and current. Each chapter covers a different topic. You can read them in any order. All of the information in it is considered best practices.

However, not every strategy will work for every author or every book. Occasionally, you might find contradicting opinions within these pages. That is to be expected. The contributors in the book bring their own skill sets, genres, and experiences to the table and may have gotten different results from the same strategy. You should pick strategies that appeal to you and experiment with them.

Book Marketing Mindset

Marketing best begins with mindset work. Through reading Dan Blank's message in the Foreword, you've already begun the journey of finding meaning and connection in your book marketing. Next, you'll find in Lisa Montanaro's chapter, "The Brand Called You! Personal & Professional Branding for Authors" a great guide for clarifying your big picture. Several later chapters in this book also delve into mindset topics. For example, Erika Lance's chapter "What is Shameless Self Promotion?" challenges authors to embrace and leverage their author celebrity status. Then Claire Fullerton reminds us, in "On Being a Good Literary Citizen," that we don't operate in a vacuum and that navigating the book community means embracing its give-and-take synergy. Following her tips for book community marketing etiquette will ensure that you come across as a professional. Finally, Katharine Herndon, Executive Director of James River Writers, shares an inspirational piece on "The Magic of Showing Up: Networking, Collaboration, and Community" that'll have you motivated to include others in your book marketing journey.

Your Book Marketing Plan

Sometimes authors get overwhelmed by book marketing. At first, they may be overwhelmed by all that they don't know. This book will help with that. But then they become overwhelmed by all that they DO know. Where should you start? What should you do next?

Enter a marketing plan. Please don't rush to launch your book. Make a plan first. Lay the foundation. You might have to change your plan. No, scratch that, you'll definitely have to change your plan somewhere along the way—life happens—but a plan will give you goals, direction, accountability, and sanity. Joelle Polisky's chapter, "Creating Your Public Relations Plan," will help you create your plan.

Marketing Strategies

I encourage you to pick and choose the marketing strategies that appeal to you. However, one non-negotiable marketing tool is your website. Every author needs a website to act as their marketing hub. Don't worry–Natalie Obando's chapter "What Every Author Should Know About Building Their Website" has you covered.

Social media is an easily accessible platform for gaining visibility, but you don't need to be a master at every platform. I recommend choosing a social media home and directing your other social media accounts there. Meredith R. Stoddard's chapter "SOCIAL Media" provides an overview of many of the popular platforms and may help you decide where to concentrate your efforts. If Facebook is where you land, then you'll find Sharvette Mitchell's chapter, "Leverage the Power of Facebook," an extremely helpful survey of all the ways you can market through Facebook.

Authors with more than one book (or planning to write more than one book) should consider building an email list. Author newsletters are the best way to transform one-time readers into lifetime fans. Rebecca Rosenberg's chapter, "Creating Effective Author Newsletters" is rich with ideas for gaining subscribers and newsletter content.

Many authors especially love interacting with readers. Participating in book events is a wonderful way to do that. Jade Dee and Wilnona Marie share book event tips in "An Eventful Day." Then Linda Ulleseit goes deeper into one particular event, an author favorite, in "Book Clubs."

Book reviews are an important component of your book's success. They provide social proof and visibility. Annie McDonnell's chapter "How to Get More Book Reviews" will give you an insider's look into securing them. If you are pitching book reviewers with book review platforms, then you'll probably need to give them a free copy of your book. At some point, though, it might feel like you are giving away more books than you are selling. Renea Winchester tackles the philosophical (and controversial) question of "How Much Should an Author Give Away?"

Once you are through the craziness of your book launch, you will likely find periods where your sales grow sluggish and you want to rekindle them. Discounting your eBook and promoting that discount is a great way to do that. My chapter, "Successful Book Promotion Strategies" gives tips for why and when to discount your eBook, then where and how to promote that discount.

Approaching This Book

Your book lives forever and so you should approach marketing like a marathon, not a sprint. If you are completely new to book marketing, you may want to read this book from cover to cover to get an overview and take notes. Then go back and take it slow, one chapter at a time, taking time to think, plan, and implement before moving on to the next chapter. If you are already experienced in book marketing, you might want to approach this book more like a resource and read the chapters you need when you need them.

In the back of the book, you'll find a free downloadable packet of resources. The packet includes the countdown lists of quick tips that follow each chapter in printable form. It also offers links to many of the resources mentioned in this anthology. Consider downloading the free packet now as you may find it helpful to have the resources handy while you read through the book.

Final Thoughts

Take a deep breath. You don't have to do it all. Make a plan. Learn and experiment. Lean into small successes and make them bigger. Abandon strategies that you can't get to work for you. Make a new plan. Write more books. Repeat. Level up.

Welcome to *Launch Pad*. Enjoy your journey to the stars!

Mary Helen Sheriff
Virginia, 2023

The Brand Called You! Personal & Professional Branding for Authors

Lisa Montanaro

Why You Need an Author Brand

"To be nobody–but yourself–in a world which is doing its best, night and day, to make you everybody else–means to fight the hardest battle which any human being can fight, and never stop fighting."
~ e. e. cummings

Whether you've finished your manuscript, are waiting for a release date, or are already in the process of marketing your book, it's never too early–or too late–to think about your author brand! With every online touchpoint and offline interaction, your author brand is being formed. Be intentional. Decide upfront what author brand story you want to tell. Branding is both how you present your books *and* yourself as a writer to the public. Aside from the obvious benefits of marketing your books and engaging with readers, developing an effective author brand can be an incredibly satisfying and creative endeavor. Developing that brand, however, requires that you be introspective and that you probe deeply to define who you are, why you write, what you write, and who you write for.

Many of us can easily identify the corporate brands of companies we are familiar with, even if we haven't purchased their products. Apple's streamlined look and simple logo, and the Nike swoosh and tagline of "Just Do It" come to mind as great examples. That type of brand identity is important in the business world for companies to set themselves apart in the marketplace.

But you're a person, why do you need a brand? Can a person be a brand? Yes! As Jeff Bezos once said: *"A brand is what other people say about you when you're not in the room."*

As an author, you are a brand. While you may not be a multinational corporation, you are indeed selling a product and you need a positive and engaging image to go with it. Your brand is how you package and present your image, and it's an essential component of marketing your writing and publications.

Being clear on your author brand will help you in immeasurable ways. You'll be able to create relevant and interesting content, better identify your ideal readers, be strategic about which social media channels to use, and determine where to spend your time and energy. Developing your author brand pushes you to decide what matters, and to say no to other opportunities based on those values. Your brand becomes like a guiding north star. It helps you take ownership of your writing career and gain control over your creative and financial future —a future that is intentionally designed and planned by you.

Branding Before Author Platform

As a writer building an author career today, regardless of the publishing path you take—traditional, small press, hybrid, or Indie—you're expected to market yourself and your books. That's where platform comes in. Author platform is simply the visibility to your target audience—building readership so you can sell your work. Author platform is heavily focused on identifying the target market of readers and how to reach them. These days, nonfiction authors are expected to have a ready-and-waiting audience. It's become somewhat of a numbers game. For fiction, it's more about writing the best book and then gathering people who will help promote your book when it publishes—your launch or street team.

Personal branding for writers is deeper than author platform. It's when you peel back the layers of the onion to get to who you are underneath before you start layering things on top of it. A lot of writers make the mistake of starting with marketing and jumping on social media, but they don't really know who they are as a writer yet. Focus first on branding and then the marketing and networking. Think of it like this:

- Branding is the Heart = the core of who you are underneath it all
- Marketing is the Skin = the part that engages with the outside world
- Networking is the Smile and Voice = the part that engages one on one, your personality brought out on a more intimate level

Writer branding is the thread that weaves itself through all your writing and books and the way you show up in the writing community. Platform tends to be specific to each book, so you may have a very different platform around each book.

For example, when my debut novel publishes in 2024, my platform will include social justice issues, LGBTQ advocacy and ally groups, my Italian heritage, being a native New Yorker, and the legal profession—all themes that show up in my manuscript. But if a subsequent book is historical fiction set in Europe, I may focus more on my European travels, my degree in political science, and the fact that I studied abroad in the Netherlands.

Thus, while you have one big, overarching author brand, you can pull out different aspects of your brand to highlight based on the marketing of each book. Then you step onto a platform and shout it from the rooftops.

What is the Brand Called You?

It's not unusual for writers to be intimidated by the business side of being an author. I'm a writer coach and when I coach authors-to-be, we almost always work on branding. Personal branding can be a vague term—it isn't just a website, a font choice, or a clever tagline. It's a blend of your skills, talents, values, interests, and beliefs reflected through your writing, online presence, and offline interactions. Your personal brand is a way of communicating what is inherently you. Your brand is mobile—you take it with you no matter where your writer career leads you. The key is to be intentional about your brand and make sure it matches who you really are and the image and reputation you want to convey.

People tend to engage with, do business with, buy from, support, and sustain relationships with those they Know, Like, and Trust. This is called the KLT Factor. Thus, people need to know you (and your writing!) to connect to the KLT. So, how do they get to know you and your writing? Through your branding.

But first, you need to know thyself! Enter the **Personal Brand Audit**.

There are four steps to the Personal Brand Audit:

Step 1: The Why of your Author Brand Identity
Step 2: Your Unique Brilliance Proposition (UBP)
Step 3: The Five Words Branding Exercise
Step 4: Your Writing Themes

We will review each step below. As we do, jot down your thoughts and answers in an author branding document, which will become the central clearinghouse of your author brand for the future.

Conduct a Personal Brand Audit

> *"Who you are speaks even louder than what you do."*
> ~ Nicolas Cole

Creating an effective author brand demands a certain level of soul-searching. You need to examine who you are, what you write, why you write it, and who you write it for—and be very clear on why this should matter to anyone else. It will help you understand the vision of your future writing career and how to best position yourself for the growth and manifestation of a successful author business.

It's not enough just to be good at what you write. You must be able to communicate your vision or the purpose behind your writing easily and clearly and coherently voice its importance to others. That's why effective branding is such a significant part of developing and growing your author platform. Aside from the obvious marketing and business benefits, developing your brand can be an incredibly creative endeavor, an introspective exercise. Think of it as an expression of you and your work—that grows and changes as you do—reflecting and showcasing your writing and the value you bring to the market.

Step 1: The why of your author brand identity

Writers are a unique mixture of artist, entrepreneur, and content creator. You've chosen this path, so you need to believe that what you write is worth writing and worth reading. Why you do what you do, as well as how you do it, informs every aspect of your author brand. Taking the time to clarify your core values and writing goals will not only aid in your marketing and promotional efforts but improve your writing as well. It's important to take a step back and look at your author career.

How do you define success as a writer and author? Your internal definition of success directly impacts your author brand. Your personal brand is not only made up of who you are, but what you stand for, and why you do what you do. Dig deep to get to the core of your brand.

Here are some probing questions to help you determine your definition of success.

- What's your big Why? What's moving you forward in your writing career? What are you doing all this for?

- Why are you a writer, and why do you write what you write?
- What's the point or purpose? What's your real end goal in pursuing a writing career?
- Do you want to sell a ton of books? Be rich or famous? See your books in the media? See your books in readers' hands? Conduct interviews or talk to book clubs?
- Do you want to build a community, start a conversation with readers about a topic, spark a movement?
- What future are you trying to create?
- How do you want to be known? What words, ideas, concepts, and feelings do you want people to associate with you? How do you want people to feel?
- What do you consistently promise to deliver? What experiences can your readers expect from you? What problems do you solve, desires do you fill, or transformations do you give to your readers?
- Why are you the one to do this? How do your values and the values of your readers converge?

Step 2: Your Unique Brilliance Proposition (UBP)

As a person—and writer—you have unique qualities that set you apart from all others. Those make up your brand. The key is to find out what they are!

What makes you stand out and sets you apart from other people and writers? What are your unique areas of brilliance?

To unearth your UBP, take inventory of the following:

- Background

- Personality
- Life experience
- Identities (nationality, cultural, ethnicity, religious, racial, gender identity, sexual orientation, marital, parental, familial, etc.)
- Geographical locations lived
- Education/degrees
- Employment
- Travel experience
- Languages spoken/accents
- Volunteer activities
- Hobbies/interests
- Passions
- Writing background and experience (publications, genre, style, voice, awards, etc.)

How are you different from everyone else? What makes you stand out in the writing community? Identify other writers in your genre and then describe what makes you different from them. Perhaps it's your experience or the way you craft a story (unique perspectives or points of view).

You'll see that you have a unique thumbprint and your UBP belongs solely to you. Start thinking about how your UBP shows up (or doesn't show up!) in your author brand. If you see important aspects of your UBP that are missing from your author brand, plan to bring them in.

This exercise is not only key to developing your author brand, but it also helps with overcoming Comparison Trap Syndrome as you realize that each writer is truly unique, and you tap into the strength of your author voice and combat Imposter Syndrome as you realize how competent you are.

Step 3: The five branding words exercise

One of my favorite ways to help determine your personal and professional brand is the Five Words Branding exercise.

In the book *Eat, Pray, Love* by Elizabeth Gilbert, every time Liz, the main character, went to a location, she tried to come up with a word to capture the brand of that location. For example, her word for Rome was Passion (or maybe it was Sex!). And at one point, someone turned the tables and asked her, "Liz, what's your word?" And she was stumped. Part of the reason she couldn't come up with her word was because she had lost touch with who she was, and needed to dig deeper, which she does as her journey progresses.

It's awfully hard to come up with just one word to describe your entire overall personal brand, so in this exercise, I'm asking you to find five words that capture what is uniquely you.

For some of you, this still may be difficult. If you can't come up with five words on your own, then pay attention to how others perceive you. Enlist the help of family, friends, writer colleagues, and publishing industry partners for five words that describe you. Please only ask those that will be your believing eyes—people who believe in what you're doing and are supportive.

Try to come up with a mix of positive words—typically adjectives—that exhibit both hard and soft skills or tap into left and right brain characteristics. We are all made up of both, so mixing up the five words for your brand is a nice way to demonstrate your multi-faceted personality and help you to appear less one-dimensional. For example, for my five words, I use three to capture more of my left-brain side and hard skills: intelligent, professional, and productive; and two to capture my more creative, right-brain side and soft skills: warm and sassy.

Make sure your words truly capture your essence, personality, and what makes you uniquely you. These words should show up in your brand online and offline and should be a good match, so if readers and others describe you, these words may come out of their mouths.

Bonus: try to come up with five branding words for each of your books and five branding words for each of your book's main characters!

Step 4: Your writing themes

Now that you've finished conducting your Personal Brand Audit, it's time to look at your writing themes. This is where your overall writer brand meets common themes in your writing.

Study your writing and try to find the through-line or sweet spot. Is there a common denominator or primary theme? Even if you write across genres, there are often elements that may tie them together. Look for consistency from book to book and pull out any patterns that appear around themes, settings, or key characteristics of characters. Try to put everything under one brand umbrella, if possible. Don't hide anything you write just because it doesn't exactly match your former or other genres. Try to brand them all if you can. Talk about the breadth of your work. You want readers to read your work just because it's written by you.

If you're self-published, brand those books along with any traditionally published books. Readers don't usually pay attention to the details of publishing–only writers and publishing industry pros typically do. If you write both fiction and nonfiction, that's okay. Look for similarities in writing style or voice, and in the themes that populate your publications. What about if you write about writing? That gives readers insight into the writing process. It shouldn't scare them off or ostracize them. It's a behind-the-scenes peek at the life of an author.

Bonus: This is super helpful when you're ready to create a tagline or slogan for your author brand.

Now It's Time to Showcase Your Brand!

You've established who you are and what makes you unique as a person and as a writer through the Personal Brand Audit, and then you've tied that to your writing themes. Now it's time to share your author brand with the world. How do you do that?

By using the **4 Cs of Author Branding**.

- Content
- Communication
- Connection
- Consistency

The First C of Author Branding: Content

One of the challenges authors struggle with is what type of branding content to share online and offline. Content will vary depending on what your unique brand is, and can include content that is educational, helpful, entertaining, or inspiring. Always aim for authentic and on-brand.

Gather Your Content Buckets

The best way to develop a content strategy is through content buckets, which are categories of topics you share the most as you document what's going on in your world. You'll share them on your website, in your blog and newsletter, during interviews, at book signings and book clubs, and on social media.

Here is a handy list:

Your Personal World

- You as a person
- Behind-the-scenes information about your personal life, family, interests, passions, hobbies, careers, travel, etc.

Your Writing World

- Process, tools, progress, community, conferences, retreats
- Your journey to writing, your journey to publishing, what you learned along the way, how you write, where you write, what you're writing next, etc. Readers like to know about your writing journey. They find it fascinating!

Your Book World

- Characters, setting, quotes, cover, themes, behind the scenes
- How you got the ideas for your books, which characters were the easiest to write, which characters were surprisingly difficult, deleted scenes, book club questions, themes in the book, research, etc.

Your Reading World

- Favorite authors, reading recommendations, book reviews, book covers, articles, blogs
- Readers love to know what you're reading, some of your favorite books, what books inspired you, what authors you admire, etc.

The Larger World

- Current events, passions, causes
- How you as an author and your book–theme, setting, story–fit into the larger world

Repurpose Content

Once you've taken the time to share fabulous content with your followers, fans, and readers, embrace the concept of repurposing content. This is when you take the same content and use it in multiple locations or in different ways. Content can be sliced and diced, expanded, and condensed. Dress it up differently based on the medium and channel. A blog post can be stripped down and shared as short social media posts. Add visuals for Instagram. Add video for other channels. Here is a handy reminder of how to repurpose content: Write it, say it, photograph it, video it!

The Second C of Author Branding: Communication

Communication is key to getting the word out about your author brand. Don't be the best-kept secret! Showcase the components of your author brand through Brand Strands.

Brand Strands

- Visual
- Auditory
- Print
- Offline
- Online

The Visual Brand Strand

A big part of your author branding will be visual: the way you look, your website, your book covers–all of those tell the story of your brand. You'll need to use colors, fonts, images, and other visual elements to convey your brand. These visual elements can express the mood of your author brand, whether that is serious, edgy, whimsical, romantic, or adventurous.

Visual components of your brand consist of:

- Physical presence
- Clothing/Style
- Hair/Makeup/Personal grooming
- Photos/Images
- Logos
- Colors
- Fonts

The Auditory Brand Strand

You are a writer and tell your stories through words. But you also have a voice. As an author, you may be a guest on podcasts and media interviews, create videos for your readers and share them on social media or your website, and hopefully do author talks, book readings, and book signings.

Auditory components of your brand consist of:

- Voice
- Speaking style
- Language/Accent
- Word choice
- Elevator pitch

The Print Brand Strand

For most authors, this is your main focus–your writing. But this brand strand goes beyond your publications. Anything that winds up in print is included. Think broadly!

Print components of your brand consist of:

- Slogan/Tagline
- Bio
- Business card/Promotional materials/Swag
- Books
- Articles/Blog posts/Social media posts/Other publications
- Writing style
- Fonts

The Offline Presence Brand Strand

While we live much of our lives engaging in online spaces these days, we still do (thankfully!) connect offline. This brand strand is made up of any in-person events, engagements, and connections.

Offline presence components of your brand consist of:

- Book clubs/Libraries/Bookstores

- Writer groups/Conferences/Workshops/Retreats
- Speaking/Teaching
- Community events

The Online Presence Brand Strand

This is the biggie–the brand strand that now takes up most authors' time, attention, and energy. The best way to maximize your online presence is to be strategic. Pay attention to who your ideal readers are and where they hang out online, and try to match that with which aspects of the online world appeal to you as well. Please note, you do not need to do all the components listed under this brand strand. And even if you do, you don't need to do them all at the same time!

Online presence components of your brand consist of:

- Website
- Blog
- Subscriber list/Newsletter
- Google Alerts of your name and book titles
- Social media profiles
- Podcasts/Interviews/Author takeovers
- Amazon/Goodreads/BookBub author profiles
- Online publications
- Professional/Writer associations' web pages
- Early reader reviews
- Author blurbs of your book

Special Considerations for the Online Brand Strand: Your Digital Footprint

Website

In my opinion, it's never too early to create a writer/author website. Not because it will land you a publishing deal, but because it helps you think of yourself as a professional and forces you to think about how to communicate what you write and why. It connects the dots. Also, having a website means you carved out a corner of the internet that is yours, and your author branding and platform get a jump start. It becomes the hub of your online world. It doesn't have to be robust to start. Build it slowly. For more about author websites see Chapter 5.

Social Media

Social media is covered in great detail in other chapters of this book. However, as it's such an important part of the online presence portion of your author brand, I couldn't resist sharing my take on the various social media channels and what makes them each unique.

- LinkedIn is like inviting someone to a business lunch or after-work networking mixer. Think professional.
- Goodreads is like inviting someone to view your private library and to talk about books.
- Pinterest is like inviting someone to view your scrapbook. Think wistful and whimsical.
- YouTube is like inviting someone to watch your private TV channel.
- TikTok is like inviting someone to watch your home movies or reality TV show.
- Instagram is like inviting someone to have lemonade on your front porch or in your back garden and the

door to the house is open, but you haven't invited them inside yet. Think surface level, but friendly.
- Facebook is like inviting someone into your living room and offering them a glass of wine or cup of coffee or tea. Think personal, colloquial.
- Twitter is like inviting someone to gather around your kitchen island where everyone else has already had too much to drink, is trying to talk at the same time, and a few family members/friends/colleagues are saying things that make you cringe, while you desperately try to get the attention of that new agent across the island. Think free-for-all.

Digital Minimalism

If you don't want a large online footprint, are a bit of a digital minimalist, are an introvert, or are very private, find an author who is similar and see what they do to connect with readers. Identify the boundaries of what you're comfortable with. Watch similar authors and even people outside the writing community to see how much they share, what they share, and how often. You can also share content that's not about you—other writers, bookstores, libraries, your charming town, a cause, etc. Think of what you're passionate about or that you want to have conversations about and focus more on that.

Balancing Privacy Concerns

When it comes to your digital footprint, use what is often referred to as the "New York Times Rule": if you wouldn't want it splashed across the front page of the newspaper, don't put it online. That includes social media!

Here are some tips and strategies for balancing privacy concerns:

- Match your social media profile handle or name to your real name or pen name, whichever you use for your author brand.
- Use Facebook "lists" creatively to protect your privacy, and keep your friends list private. Also, pay attention to the privacy setting of your posts and select which are to be shared with the public or friends only.
- Don't post photos that identify the outside of your home, street name, or house number.
- Use location/geotag after the fact.
- Don't post identifying photos of your children if you don't feel comfortable with that.
- Make your Instagram profile public. A private one is not going to further your author brand.

Balancing a Day Job or Business with your Author Brand

If you have a day job, run a business, or any other type of side hustle that is non-author related, you must make some decisions as to whether you'll have separate online presences–one for your author brand and one for your non-author career. If you can have a comprehensive online presence and incorporate all sides of your personal and professional life, it's a lot easier, cleaner, and more productive–and less work, as you don't need to maintain double the number of websites and social media accounts. Thus, when you can, opt for the WYSIWYG approach–what you see is what you get!

However, this approach won't be the best match for every author. Some authors may need separate brands for their author career and non-author career. Be strategic when choosing which social media platforms you use for each.

The Third C of Author Branding: Connection

When it comes to author branding, try not to lose sight of genuine connection. Think of your brand as an opportunity to have a deeper internal conversation that says who you are on many levels. Don't miss that opportunity! Welcome that conversation. Show up and be present. Truly engage with people. Champion other authors and writers, connect to and get to know readers, reviewers, and book influencers. Always aim for authentic, polite, and on-brand.

Find other authors who are rocking their author brand. Study their websites, social media profiles, newsletters, and more. Watch what they share and how they interact with readers and others, and then model your behavior after them using your own brand, of course.

The Fourth C of Author Branding: Consistency

Creating, refining, and consistently presenting your author brand is a core part of your author career. Stay committed to your brand and be consistent with your content, communication, and connection. When you stray too far, it leads to disjointed messaging and can appear inauthentic, confuse your readers, or in the worst-case scenario, even turn them off.

Your brand may naturally evolve as you experience different phases of an author career—pre-published, querying and submissions phase, pre-launch phase, launch phase, post-launch phase, and multiple books published phase. Where do you see your author career in one year, three years, and five years? Does your brand match your author career for the long haul, or will it need to be tweaked? Use the phases of your author career as an opportunity to rethink your brand at every step along the way.

Launch the Brand Called You!

After completing your Personal Brand Audit, you know who you are as an author, why you write, and what you write. And you've learned the 4 Cs of Author Branding, so you're equipped to showcase your brand to the world. You have all you need to launch the brand that is you.

You've got this. I'm cheering you on with a glass of Prosecco in hand. Now, go launch that brand!

Top Ten Countdown to Launching Your Author Brand

Remember, it doesn't matter what stage of your author career you're in. Even if you're already published, it's never too late to think about branding. Ideally, though, you should address branding in the pre-publishing phase of your author journey. Try not to leave branding for when your book is getting ready to launch and scramble at the last minute. Start early!

10. Create an author branding document to serve as a central clearinghouse for your branding content to use throughout your writing career as you build, share, and change your brand. You can use a Word doc, a note on your smartphone, or a notes app.

9. Create a photo album on your smartphone and computer to capture images for author branding.

8. Get a graphic design account for creating attention-grabbing images and visuals that promote your author brand. Canva and Book Brush are good choices.

7. Find author comps for branding purposes. Watch, study, learn, and emulate.

6. Create a tagline or slogan that captures your author brand.

5. Claim your domain name. Your name.com is ideal. If you can't get it, add on "Writer," "Author," or "Books."

4. Take up online real estate by creating a website. That's the hub of your author brand. You own that content.

3. Start a subscriber list/newsletter. These are the people that have raised their hands and want to hear from you in their email inboxes.

2. Create a note on your phone, computer, or in a notes app for content buckets and start adding to it. Capture things happening in your personal world, writing world, reading world, book world, and the larger world to share as part of your author brand. You can organize the content into an editorial calendar to be even more strategic as to what, when, and where to share in the future.

1. Repurpose content. Write it, say it, photograph it, video it. Dress it up differently based on the medium and channel.

Meet Lisa Montanaro

Lisa Montanaro is part no-nonsense Italian American New Yorker and part sunny Californian. She has a unique background as a performer, teacher of deaf students, recovered lawyer, coach, speaker, and author. Her book, *The Ultimate Life Organizer: An Interactive Guide to a Simpler, Less Stressful & More Organized Life*, was published in 2011. Lisa's debut novel, a dual-timeline family drama, will be published by Red Adept Publishing in 2024. Lisa serves as Webinar Host for the Women's Fiction Writers Association (WFWA). As a Branding, Business, Mindset, and Productivity Coach for writers, Lisa provides support for all stages of a writing career.

Website: https://lisamontanarowrites.com/

Creating Your Public Relations Plan
Joelle Polisky

So, you wrote your book, and it's being published! Congratulations!

Now what?

Your goal now is to promote your book so that it is purchased, read, and talked about by raving fans. This goal is universal and applies whether you are traditionally published or not. With the publishing world changing at such a rapid pace, fewer and fewer public relations services come with a traditional publishing contract. Increasingly, across all markets, it is the author and their public relations plan that leads to break-out success. In this chapter, I am going to walk you through some critical steps in creating a plan that can be vital to your success. Believe me, having a public relations plan is VITAL. Without one, very few will know your book even exists.

Have you heard of the "Seven Times Rule"? It means a prospective customer needs to hear or see a message at least seven times before they will take action. In your case as an author, to buy your book. Enter your public relations plan—the thing that gets your name and your book in front of people. Public relations (PR) cannot be an afterthought. It's important to get exposure for your book.

I am a firm believer that you should create a roadmap to gain attention for your book prior to publication. Better yet, you should develop your PR plan as you are writing your book. Map out all the tasks on a timeline so it is easy to check them off your list and still balance this PR work with the writing life you love. The plan should include action steps that start 4-6 months before your publication date because editors and producers of many media outlets work on long lead times. They are working on content up to 6 months in advance of when articles go to print. Therefore, you are unlikely to be chosen for interviews or media requests if you start your PR campaign after your book launch date or even too far in advance. The reality is that most of the larger media editors won't even consider you for a story if they receive your pitch and your book after your launch date.

It's a sad reality, but unless there is a compelling news angle related to your book, your book will be "old news" quickly after launch. Years of PR work tell me that the ideal time to start your launch plan is six months before the release date for your best results. However, it's not impossible to reach success even if you are starting late. We will address that toward the end of the chapter. For now, know that I've worked with authors who have achieved great success with their books and in expanding their author careers, but not without a plan.

Marketing vs. Public Relations

It's helpful to draw a distinction between marketing and public relations. Generally, "marketing" handles anything with regard to paid promotion (advertisements, book promotions, participating in book fairs, development of "swag" like bookmarks and other giveaway items, and the like). Public relations, on the other hand, targets "earned" media. Public relations strategies focus on acquiring press coverage and interviews through media outlets such as television, radio, blogs, social media, newspapers, and magazines. Public relations is about creating relationships between you, the media, and an audience.

In truth, you will need a plan that includes both marketing and public relations as we've described them here. For this chapter, we will focus on public relations, earned media. Ultimately, having a successful public relations campaign provides credibility to you as an author and speaks to how serious you are about your book. However, many authors believe PR is the be-all and end-all in getting book *sales*. That is not the purpose of PR! The purpose of PR is to get you in front of your targeted audience to sell yourself, have the audience become interested in you and your work, and sell books. A well-thought-out public relations campaign does just that.

Promoting your book can require full-time dedication. Handling all the tasks yourself requires a lot of time and effort. As you read through this chapter, and indeed this book, make note of the elements of marketing and public relations that appeal to you, overwhelm you, pique your interest to learn more, and those you know you need help with. Those notes will lead you to know whether you want to engage a public relations team for some or all of this work.

PR Campaign Nuts and Bolts

Let's walk through the steps and items you will need to have on hand even before you create the step-by-step timeline for your PR plan. I know that if you are like most authors, you do not necessarily crave the spotlight or have the desire to do this work yourself. However, there are some elements of the work that, regardless whether you hire a PR team or not, you will have to work out for yourself. Knowing, for example, the first two items below, and clearly communicating your thinking to a PR team, will save time and money and result in a better plan.

Let's get started!

Identify Why You Wrote the Book. Do you just want to sell books? Achieve book awards? Perhaps it's to help boost your business or champion a cause. Knowing your goal will allow you to create story angles and identify the type of events and media outlets you should pursue.

Identify Your Audience. This is so important in the promotion of your book. Is your book a children's book, a thriller, or perhaps a book geared toward cat lovers who live in Ireland? Is there a specific demographic that will resonate with your book? Knowing your specific target audience will further help in knowing what media outlets to pursue.

Plan and Create Your Messaging. This has something to do with author branding, as you will read in other chapters, but it's also book specific. What makes your book unique? What are the major themes? How do you want to move or persuade your audience?

Create a Book Synopsis or Short Overview. This is the "elevator pitch" for your book. During interviews, you will have under 30 seconds to tell what your book is about. The book overview is the perfect opportunity to tell potential readers why they need to buy and read your book. Many authors tell me the hardest part of writing their book was the back cover book blurb. Start there and then whittle the elevator pitch to just 30 seconds.

Create Your Author Website. Your website can be elaborate or as simple as one landing page. Refer to the chapter on websites in this book for detailed information. Here, know that many times, your website will be the first place an editor or producer will go to see if you are a seriously legitimate author dedicated to your craft and platform.

Create a Press Release. A good press release will include all the information needed for a reporter about your event. Similar to the sell sheet, it has to have a wow factor. But unlike the sell sheet, it is targeted for one specific event. Yes, you should have one for your launch, but also for your launch party and any other newsworthy event like a fundraiser or a media appearance. You can also create a press release connecting a theme or topic in your book to a current event, trending fad, or hot topic. A typical press release includes:

- Catchy headline
- Media angle(s)
- Synopsis
- Comparable book titles and/or authors
- Contact information
- Cover image
- Publication date
- Publisher
- Price

Create a Sell Sheet. This is your one-page, wow, press release-type sheet that ignites the reader to say yes to your request for media attention. The sell sheet has two target audiences. One is important for sales and acquisitions by libraries, retailers, and wholesalers. This is, perhaps, the most common use of the sell sheet. The other important audience, particularly as it relates to this chapter, is the media. While there are critical elements to the sell sheet, the most important one is the hook that captures the editor's or producer's attention, making them see that this author, this story, and this book is the right match for my organization. The hook that you develop will talk about your book but also why you are the right fit. Something along the lines of "in a politically charged social climate this book transcends politics and brings readers together to fight for a shared moral victory" or "with the heart-warming theme of home for the holidays this book captures your soul and takes you back in time to the Christmas of . . ." You get the idea. Using reviews as a hook is also a successful practice. The rest of the sell sheet usually includes:

- Book overview
- Author bio
- Author headshot
- Image of book
- Publisher
- ISBN # (if your book has multiple ISBNs, identify and enumerate them)
- Price of book in the various formats
- # of pages, length for listening, etc.
- Book category/genre
- Launch date

Create a Media Kit. The content included in the media kit is much the same as what you've created for your website. Media Kits are sent to editors/producers of media outlets to entice them to learn about you and your book and to convince them to feature you in their outlet. As just mentioned, you'll want all this on your website as well. Here's what you will want to include:

- Sell sheet
- Synopsis of your book
- Author bio, both a short and a long version (think one is to inform an interviewer, the other might be used to introduce you)
- Author image (formal headshots are important but don't be afraid to have some more candid shots as well)
- Book cover image
- Where to buy your book
- Book reviews
- Press release
- Book trailer (if you have one)
- Q and A with questions they might like to ask you and your answers
- Key themes, trends, connections to current events
- Contact information

Set Up Author Social Media Pages. Minimally, create a Facebook author page, Instagram profile, and LinkedIn presence. Depending on your genre and target audience, you will want to go beyond these to TikTok (available at the time we go to press) and other platforms relevant to your work. In addition to your author website, social media platforms are where editors and producers will turn to learn more about you as an author and your book. It is important to post regularly on these platforms, and it's critical to interact with people who respond to your posts.

Submit Your Book for Reviews. Of course, you will want your author friends to read and review your book. Reviews are the lifeblood of successful books. You will also want to engage with your readers across social media and solicit their reviews. However, in my experience, having a book review from a credible outlet is a huge win for an author. That's why you see so many of these reviews painted across book covers and social media posts. Professional book reviews increase your visibility and establish trust with your potential audience. Some reviews are free and some have an associated cost. Others still are what we call *advertorials*. Here, think infomercial. An advertorial review is basically an advertisement that looks like a review. For now, know that there are editorial reviews that legitimately assess your work and those that are more of an advertisement.

There are some important things to note about professionally curated reviews that will also impact your planning timeline. As you consider reviewers, you will learn that some reviewers can take nearly 2-3 months to return a review. If you want a review by the launch date, this means you will need to apply and have advanced reader copies (ARC) available as well. Additionally, you want to consider that even when you pay for a review, there is no guarantee that it will be a positive review. That is how it should be. In seeking and receiving reviews from professional reviewers, you must be aware of their terms and conditions before you post their review. In many cases, you must post the entire review, not just a certain element. So, for example, if a reviewer states "one of the most fascinating books I've read this year" and then goes on to criticize or pan the book, you may or may not be entitled to post the first part of the review without the second part. Just a word to the wise.

Source Media Outlets. Source or identify the media outlets you'd like to pitch in order to get featured. You are looking for outlets that include articles, Q & As, interviews, reviews, blogs, and book briefs. These should include local and national TV, radio, newspapers, podcasts, and blogs. Most local newspapers and morning television shows are interested in local stories and have shorter lead times. Magazines have the longest lead time of up to six months. Podcasters tend to be more interested in stories and themes that will transcend simply your book launch. They want shows that contain information that their listeners will always find useful.

Go back to your why and target audience here in order to make your media list.

Does your book have strong themes about child abuse or assault–how can you tie that to national campaigns? Does your book take place in a specific local coffee shop, town, etc.? How can you tie that to the Chamber of Commerce? Is your novel historical fiction? What organizations champion the era you write about? Making these kinds of connections between you and your book and localities and organizations is what makes you all the more appealing to media outlets.

Make a List of Potential Author Events. Where can you provide an author reading? Who is interested in author talks? Contact local libraries, literary festivals, alumni publications, industry affiliations, rotary clubs, book clubs, retirement homes, schools, civic organizations, and historical societies. Consider the range of topics you can speak to, beyond focusing on "just" your book. You can talk about your publishing journey and what you learned. You may now be an expert on multiple topics based on the research you've done for your book. I know one author who has mastered spinning yarn and other materials based on research she did for her novel. She even owns multiple spinning wheels, opening a whole range of speaking opportunities for her to talk about spinning, but also her book.

Create Goodreads and BookBub Author Pages. Their programs allow published authors to create a profile page to promote their book and engage with readers. Once you are verified by these platforms, ask your readers to follow you here and leave reviews. These two sites are the current industry leaders, but depending on your genre and how far you want to take your public relations planning, you will want to explore and be involved in other sites as well. Keep in mind that, as in most of this work, you will be most successful if you engage, comment, and follow others on these platforms.

Now Let's Set a Tight Timeline

Everything you've already read about should be planned for and carried out in the four to six months before your launch. Now, we are getting close and a lot more has to happen in months three and beyond.

Three Months Prior to Launch

- Edit and finalize all the items we have laid out above. Pay special attention to your sell sheet, press release, and elevator pitch. Keep the pitch brief and exciting to attract the attention of the editor. Practice your pitch orally so you are ready to give it, regardless of what question you are asked in an interview.

- Contact critical media outlets. As listed earlier, depending on the media outlet, editors may be planning their content 4-6 months ahead. Forward your book/author pitch along with your media kit, requesting an interview or book blurb to share with their audience. Make sure to include a link to all of this and your author website.
- Have physical copies of your book ready to send out to interested media outlets and potential advanced readers. Depending on your publishing method, you will also have access to a variety of electronic formats of your book. You will need to learn about these formats and how to transmit them, as well as the widely used Book Funnel program.
- Work and create posts on your social media platforms to show you are active and engaged and someone people are interested in. Develop a plan for your posts that share about you and your book. Remember, interaction across social media platforms is key.

One Month Before Launch

- Follow up with media outlets and finalize interview dates with long leads.
- Distribute and reach out to local radio and newspapers.
- Host a cover reveal. You can do this on your website and your social media platforms. This will get readers excited about your soon-to-be-launched book.
- Plan a Book Launch Party. Invite your friends, family, and colleagues, and also include the media. In recent years, we have seen these done both in real life and virtually. Regardless of the virtual or live format,

consider the venue. If you write historical fiction, is there a historic locale that is suitable? Have a coffee shop in your book? Will a local coffee shop host you? Be prepared to sell books, do a reading, welcome well-wishers, and more. Be prepared for what it means to sell your books in various venues. You'll need to be a bit savvy about any required taxes–both in terms of collection and reporting, as well as how you will collect monies, provide change, accept electronic payments, and more. While book swag falls more directly under your marketing plan, there's no denying that swag also endears you to readers and the media. Consider the costs of each of these elements like, venue, swag, receipt of payments, mailings, and more in your overall thinking regarding your launch.

Launch Week and Beyond

- Host your Launch Party. Friends, family, and colleagues will help you celebrate the debut of your new book. But what to do at the party? Read an excerpt from your book. Set up a place to sign books. Create photo ops with the author. Have a contest or game related to your content. Think about demonstrations that might be linked to your theme. If the book contains a circus theme, you might have face painting. You are a writer; you create worlds. Create a book launch to be remembered. Also, take pictures at your party to include on your social media platforms.
- Post! Post! Post on your social media platforms! Share pictures of the physical book. Keep your followers updated on any media coverage and reviews you've

received. Remember to tag and thank the media outlets that cover your event.
- Continue media outreach to gain additional media coverage.
- Create a newsletter to send to family and friends and new followers.
- Write guest posts and articles for other authors or bloggers to be posted on their sites.
- Host a "live" event on your socials. Share your launch, and combine your launch with other authors. You want to make your presence known and live videos are a great way to attract new readers.
- Keep your goals in mind. You likely imagine yourself on Good Morning America and your book as a Netflix series, and you should. But success builds on success. Start local, catalog your success, send thank you notes, and keep your website current with the media attention and reviews you receive. Follow up with contacts in which you have a particular interest. A note on following up vs. being a pest. You should absolutely continue to reach out to media contacts. Remember, this is about relationships! But, pace your contacts, and maybe curb your enthusiasm. You want to keep yourself and your book at the top of the mind of the media outlet. This is best accomplished when you have something newsworthy to report. Reaching out too often with the same news runs you the risk of being blocked by the contact.

Oops, I Didn't Do All That and My Book is Out!

The truth of the matter is some authors realize after their launch that they would have been more successful had they followed a plan. I've also seen authors start their plan too soon with the effect that potential readers have already moved on to their next great read by the launch date. So let's take a minute to look at what you can do to ignite or reignite enthusiasm about your book, even after it launches.

You'll still want to have all the items in your tool kit that we've already discussed: the sell sheet, media kit, website, etc. so take time to create them now. If you are starting late, your social media engagement and hook matter all the more.

The more you engage on social media, not only on your own social media pages but in groups and other author pages, the more you will get noticed. Comment, comment, comment. Offer to guest blog. Participate in multiple ways. One of my clients calls all this "sucking up." It works. You will build a community of readers and authors who look forward to your participation. Consider how you post on your pages and be generous with your praise of others. Build a schedule for your posts that is a balance between your personal life (for you to decide how much and what you wish to share), promotion of your book specifically, and themes related to your book. It's helpful to remember to always ask a question in your post. This encourages followers to not simply scroll but to actually interact with you and with each other.

Now for the hook, and this is important. You want to think, similar to what we've already mentioned, about why you are the perfect guest blogger, interview guest, or featured author. Develop a list of these hooks related to your book but also to you and the author brand you want to develop and hone. If your book is about reinventing yourself, seek out blogs and podcasts that focus on that. If your book is about families, find those platforms. Keep your current events awareness high. If something happens in your local or world news that is a specific match for your book, contact the reporter who wrote or reported the story and share why you are particularly relevant at this time.

You might also want to consider a virtual book tour. These are popular both when books launch and as part of book anniversary celebrations (yes, those are real things and should be planned for as well). There are PR professionals who specialize solely in creating virtual book tours that come with reviews and interviews. Frequently, these professionals contract for a flat rate for a certain number of interviews or reviews, usually on social media platforms.

It's also important to remember that what will sell your current book most may very well be your next book. Planning for the next one, publicizing this one, and writing are the trifecta of the modern author's success.

Phew! Deep Breath. Do I Go It Alone?

While the above may be overwhelming, it is all doable. But it also reflects just some of the tasks used to highlight and promote your book to others. It is extremely time-consuming and doesn't give you much time to do what you love–WRITE.

Whether you do it yourself or hire a publicist, there is no right or wrong path. It boils down to if you're willing and able to handle all the tasks involved yourself and how much are you willing and able to spend. While these are the two factors you are most likely to consider, there is more to the PR/author formula. Beyond the task list accomplishment and media connections, there is something more that you want from any publicist you hire. A relationship. As we mentioned elsewhere, this entire public relations aspect of your work is about relationships. A good publicist will handle all the details and business of getting your book in front of others to allow you to focus on the writing. But a great publicist is your #1 cheerleader. A publicist that empowers you and keeps you on track, making sure those most important know about your book. A good publicist also builds a strong rapport with you, the author. They help motivate and educate you on the tools and venues to best get your book the attention it deserves. They help you develop a media presence and serve as your media coach. A great publicist helps you adhere to a schedule, engage with your audience, boost your book, and WRITE MORE!

How do you find the right publicist? The best starting place is to talk with other authors. You can find out costs and deliverables and successes and challenges. Ask about each of these. You can look to the popular Upwork, Fiverr, and LinkedIn as places to start your search if you don't have author connections, but without a face-to-face connection you are unlikely to get to the important intangible of "can this person make magic happen for me."

As with any contracting, you will want to review the terms of any PR contract you are considering. Some publicists will offer a specific time period in which specific deliverables can be guaranteed, like your press kit, website, etc., but the intangibles will be your actual media coverage. If a publicist guarantees you media placements—run, do not work with them. A great publicist will never give you such a promise. Why may you ask? Because there are so many variables out of your control and theirs. Trying to get media coverage depends on the regular workload of a reporter, including if they get redirected to cover a story in place of yours, if something more newsworthy is happening, etc. Your publicist may have some givens and guarantees, and those you should know about upfront. They may also pose opportunities for advertorials, as we discussed under reviews above, but keep in mind this is not *earned* media and as such, they provide far less credibility, not to mention the costs can creep into whatever budget you have in mind for this area of your book promotion.

Lastly, a note about costs. Even though I have been in the business for over 25 years, I am still amazed at the PR costs that some authors incur. It is not unheard of for authors to pay upwards of $15,000 for PR services. Yes, you can spend less, or not use a publicist. What is important is that you go into this phase of the work with your eyes wide open, an eye on your budget, and an understanding that the PR work does not necessarily translate into book sales. I prefer to work in package increments with clear benchmarks and expectations. I prefer to be the cheerleader for my clients and help them grow their author business organically as well. If we are honest, most authors are not going to be earning six-figure incomes, at least at the start. So managing your money as you approach the work of marketing and publicizing your book, and all at the same time writing your next books, is something I urge you to consider. You are a vital part of the success of your book, including in marketing and publicizing it. You've got this!

Top Ten Countdown to a Successful Public Relations Campaign

Your author success will depend in large measure on your own marketing and public relations efforts. There is a formula that can be followed and you, or you and your publicist, can make success happen.

10. Set your goals and know your audience.

9. Determine if you want to engage a PR professional in some or part of this work.

8. Build a tool kit of materials, including your media kit and sell sheet.

7. Practice your elevator speech.

6. Develop your PR plan.

5. Source media contacts.

4. Become active on social media.

3. Develop strategies for engagement and hooks beyond the world of your book.

2. Enjoy your launch.

1. Continue to build your media presence and keep yourself and your book relevant to build on your well-earned success.

Meet Joelle Polisky

Joelle began her 25-year PR career working with professional athletes and premiere sporting events through Advantage International. She's worked at several PR agencies to get major media placements for clients across industries. Joelle's coverage for clients includes *The Today Show, Good Morning America,* and the cover of *Newsweek*; but like a good PR professional, she knows that it's important to focus on strategic hits that will provide the most benefit for clients, whether it's a local daily paper or a podcast or the newest media trend.

Website: http://goshiftkey.com/

What is Shameless Self-Promotion?

Erika Lance

Before that question is answered, I want to tell you why you may be inclined to listen to me on this topic. To start, I am a published author and the CEO of 4 Horsemen Publishing and Accomplishing Innovation Press. I also host the podcast *Drinking with Authors*, where I have spoken with hundreds of authors on their journeys to success. It has been my huge honor to speak at writing and publishing events on this topic, and now I am fortunate to share this with you.

What is Shameless Self-Promotion? In order to answer that question, you, as an author, must first understand a couple of things:

- The moment you publish a book, you are a celebrity.
- Now that you are a celebrity, you need to make sure you create your brand for your business.

You might be thinking that publishing a book doesn't make you a "celebrity." If you are of the mind that in order to be considered a "celebrity," you have to be an author like Stephen King, Neil Gaiman or Stephenie Meyer, to put it simply: you are wrong.

You are a PUBLISHED AUTHOR!!

The moment that your book is available for pre-order or when it is published, you have attained celebrity status. The only thing you have to decide is how big of a celebrity you want to be. Let those words sink in for a moment.

Another mindset that you need to have is that you are now in the business of selling your books. Again, it doesn't matter how you are published–*you* are going to be expected to be a big part of your success.

The other side of this yin/yang of your celebrity status is that you are also a brand. It is vital that as you move forward in this adventure, you keep in mind that *you* are what will decide the level of success you have as an author.

Let's go back to the title of this chapter. Shameless Self-Promotion simply means that you are willing to talk about and actively share about you as an author and your books at **any opportunity** that you can. You never know if the next barista you are talking to will turn into a huge fan of your work. Never assume anything about your potential readership. Be shameless about it and willing to put yourself out there.

From this moment on, if you have not done this already, I want you to walk into any situation with confidence, knowing that you are a published author, a celebrity, and a big deal. People *want* to read the work you are producing, and you must always assume this to be true. Do not think you have to have a big ego in order for this to work. You don't and quite frankly, you shouldn't. However, you can have the confidence or put on your confidence suit because you, the author, are all the things I have stated. You are amazing, and there is no room for shyness about how great your work is.

One of the biggest overlooked components of doing anything new is actually learning how to do it. You're reading this book, which is a good step; however, do not underestimate the importance of always learning. There are podcasts, seminars, writer's groups, writer's forums and tons of books, like this one, on the various subjects of promoting you as an author and your books. Knowledge is power! Always continue to learn and find what works for you. You do not have to do it all; you simply have to find what works for you and comfortably grow it.

I meet authors all the time who tell me that the one thing that surprised them the most, regardless of how they were published, is how much work it takes to get their book into the hands of readers. This is true–it is work. This does not mean you will not succeed. Just start where you feel the most comfortable and build from there. You can do this!

An interesting fact that may surprise you is that in the last ten years the two most common ways a book finds an audience is word of mouth and author platform. Advertising is not even a close third to these powerhouses. Spending a bunch of money for advertising is not the best first step to get your book in the hands of your audience. I am not saying to not do ads; I am saying that you can invest your time and resources into these two things and possibly get some pretty amazing results. Let's dive into how you make that happen.

Author Platform

I am going to begin with how to accomplish your author platform. When you start in earnest building word of mouth, you need to have somewhere to direct people.

Social Media

Let's start with social media and decide on what handle to use. The biggest thing to remember is you will have to say the handle to people when doing podcasts, public speaking, at booths where you are selling or signing your books, and of course, anytime when you are talking about your writing. People will want to know where to find you.

You may already have social media and be thinking you can just use those. However, I will point out again that as a published writer/celebrity, your life is now open to the public and strangers may look you up. How much personal information do you want out there? The bigger the celebrity (aka more popular) you become, the more you may want to keep hidden. This is not meant to scare you but instead to make you look to the future and what your goals are as a writer, instead of what is in front of you right now.

You do not want to choose something that is so complex or hard to spell that the potential fan has no way of finding you. I will use myself as an example. I write under my name: Erika Lance. The main genre I write in is Horror/Suspense (besides nonfiction). I ended up choosing @AuthorELance for my handles and www.erikalance.com for my website. This was to make it easy to tell people how to find me.

Some examples of what not to do:

- @Erikalancebooksandwriting (Way too long!)
- @ErikaLanceAuthor1287 (This seems like I couldn't get the name I wanted, so I added numbers.)
- @Erikalikescannedsoup (This is whimsical, but not easy for fans to find you.)
- @Ilovemydogsally (What does this have to do with what I write?)

I could list a hundred different examples of what *not* to do; instead, let's talk about what to do. Most fans will try to find you by your name in search engines like Google and on different social media platforms. Try to use your name (or first initial and last name) as part of your handle. You can add "Author," "Writes," "Books," or something similar if needed because your name is taken. Search the platforms for the handle you want to use before you use it. Search Facebook pages, Twitter, Instagram, TikTok, websites, and any others you might use such as Patreon, Discord, Tumbler, etc. Search for the domain name. You can easily do this on a platform such as godaddy.com. When you find a version of the handle and the domain name you want to use on all platforms, then snag it. You can create the accounts without loading them with content, but reserving your name for potential future use. Don't forget to get an email for your author contact. Do not use your personal email for the reasons listed above. If you can, find something like LinkTree, which allows you to store all your social media and websites in one place. This way, you can create one QR code for people to reach you anywhere.

Now that you have the names, what do you do with them? I have my personal/professional opinion on the correct steps to take next. But remember, you need to find what works best for you.

Creating your Brand

Logo: You have your author name. You can create a logo that goes with it or find someone on fivver.com or another site. Heck, you may know someone who does graphics. But create something you believe will stand for some time. You want something people will recognize when they see it on a banner or any other marketing material.

Headshot: You do not have to pay someone to do a headshot for you. Most of us have amazing cameras right in the palms of our hands. If you can get someone else in your life to take the photo, that is better than a selfie, but use what you can. When taking a headshot, however, you want it to be at a mostly straight-on angle, mid-chest on up, good lighting, fairly plain background, basic colors in your clothes, and a nice look on your face. Taking one outside with nature in the background is good. You should be the only person in the shot. Do not edit with all kinds of filters. They simply want to see you.

Bio: You need basically two different bios: one short and one long. I would suggest reading the bios of your favorite authors to get a feel for it. Remember that your bio is talking about you in the third person, not first.

Website: There are many free ways to do this, such as WordPress, Squarespace, GoDaddy, HubSpot, Blue Host, Wix, etc. You do not need to pay a bunch of money to get your website up and running. If you need help, there are tons of educational materials. Never underestimate the power of searching YouTube videos on the how-to of anything.

Buy links: Make sure you always have the links to buy your books on your website. You can use books2read.com to help you get one link that leads to the many vendors that will be selling your books, depending on how you are published. ALWAYS make sure people can buy books from your website.

Newsletter: There are a few sites where you can do this like Constant Contact, Hubspot, Mailchimp, GoDaddy, etc. There are again tons of educational material on how to do this. It is a vital part of your brand for reviews and purchases.

Business cards: I feel like a business card is one of the most important things you can have as an author. The only rule I believe is that you should keep it simple. Your logo or name on the front, your socials (or QR Code), and how to sign-up for your newsletter on the back. You do not have to spend a lot of money on this. If you want to be whimsical, you can have them be square or round. I had round cards when I first ordered them and people used them as coasters and always commented on it.

Socials: This means starting with the socials you feel the most comfortable to set-up. You can use your logo and at least start with a simple set-up. To get ideas on how to do this, check out some of your favorite authors (bonus if they write in the same genre as you), and see what you like about their set-up and create something similar. If you decide to create a Facebook page, then consider creating a group for your fans too. Come up with a fun name for it. This will come in super handy for many things, but most importantly, it is a way for you to interact with your fans. Jonathan Maberry does an Ask-Me-Anything with his fans almost every Thursday.

TikTok: Also, if you venture into TikTok, you should know that TikTok fans expect you to post daily. Also, TikTok fans are super big on gimmicks. An example of this is an account where a person rolls a D20 (a twenty-sided dice) to determine what kind of sandwich they are going to make. They roll for the bread, cheese, meat, etc and have over 200K in fans. If you are going to do TikTok, block off the time to do it and find something fun you can do that ties into your writing.

Author pages: Make sure you set-up your author page on Goodreads and Amazon (Author Central). This way, you can add your books together under your pen name and collect reviews. Your readers can also be notified when you have a new book available for pre-order.

Elevator pitch: You should, when asked, in fifteen seconds, be able to describe your book. You want to have a simplified blurb that includes genre and why someone would want to grab it immediately.

More Shameless Self-Promotion

Make sure you have business cards on you at ALL TIMES! This is in caps because it is so important. I do not care if you are getting gas, going to Walmart at two in the morning in your pajamas, or getting your teeth cleaned–take your business card! You will find that you will talk about your writing and books more than you know. If you are anywhere and someone asks what you do, YOU ARE A WRITER, and if you still have a day job mention that second. They will immediately ask you what you write: BAM, hand them your card. I may have used a bunch of caps in this paragraph, but I cannot stress this enough: TAKE YOUR BUSINESS CARDS EVERYWHERE!

You may be wondering if you should get bookmarks or pens or even bags with your logo on it. The answer is simple: no. You do not have to spend money on all of that to market yourself and your book. Remember, you are a business now. If you think someone won't read your book if you do not give them a pen or bookmark, you are mistaken. I have seen authors spend a ton of money, and it simply will not increase your book sales. Even when you set-up to sell or do book signings, you still do not need these. You need signage and a pen to sign books (and of course–business cards).

After you are set up with a place to guide your throngs of fans, let's talk about how to find them. The list below captures just some ideas on where to find your fans, and how to bring awareness to you and your books.

Word-of-Mouth

Find your kindred: Since writing is such a solitary sport in a way, it is important to find a group of other authors with which to collaborate. This can be done as a writing/critique group–be careful to find one that you feel comfortable with and is supportive; if they are not, move on to the next until you find one. Reach out to other authors in your genre. I have found that authors can truly be some of the nicest people. You just have to reach out. Search for writing meet-ups, writing events, and publishing conferences in your area. You will meet other authors and you might find some of your new best friends.

Open mics: I know that sometimes reading out loud in front of people is terrifying. However, as you become more and more famous, your fans will want this. Also, it is a great place to meet new writer friends and fans. I actually met my writing partner for a series at an open mic. It also lets you see how your WIP (work in progress) goes over with a live audience.

Podcasts: There are several podcasts that have authors on to discuss their books and writing. Almost all will want a bio, headshot, socials, and images of your book covers. I would create a little digital folder that contains all of this that you keep up-to-date. Depending on what type of writer you are, you might want to wait to do podcasts until you have a couple of books under your belt. Yes, you can work on selling your first book, but you make more money off having multiple book sales, and some podcasts might only have you on the one time. If you go on to talk about book number three people may buy the other two books when they see how great the first one is. Some podcasts have you put down a deposit in case you cancel on them. This is okay. If they want you to pay to be on the podcast, you may want to hold off and speak to other authors who have been on the podcast to see if it made a difference for them in sales. You are a business owner; it has to be worth the expense.

Book clubs: Finding local and virtual book clubs (you can find some in your local libraries) and reaching out to them as an author can be fantastic. Several book clubs love to have the authors pop-in, even virtually, to discuss their book. This is a great word-of-mouth tool.

Fan page takeovers: This is when you connect with other authors in your genre or one similar, which you can and should do on all platforms, and you take turns taking over each other's fan groups. The truth is that no matter how prolific of a writer you are, you will never keep up with your fans as far as the amount they can consume. So, how do you fix this? You create a group of authors and keep the fans fed and connected so that when your next book comes out, they are already clicking the BUY button when it is on pre-order or live.

Newsletter swaps: Another way to leverage relationships with other authors of your genre or similar genres is to feature each other in your newsletters with links and information. This is again a great way to feed your fans books and also expand your newsletter base by linking with other authors' fans.

ARCs (Advance Reader Copies) for reviews: On your webpage, you may want to offer readers an ARC in return for a review. Services like BookSprout can help you to do this as well. This is a great strategy if you have a book on pre-order.

Local markets: Most of us have local markets or art fairs in our area. Booths at these are often inexpensive, under $50. Check out the crowds beforehand and ask other vendors how they do there. But they can be fun and an easy way to find some new fans.

Libraries: Go into your local library and speak to the librarian about how to get your book into the library. You may have to supply your book to them, depending on how you are published.

Local bookstores: Go to your local mom and pop shops and find out what it would take to stock your book and even do a book signing. Even if you have to bring your books with you, see if they will advertise it with the promotion you supply. This will get your local fan base engaged. Also, you can always ask to do a book release party with them.

Everything I have mentioned is not everything that you can do as an author. As I stated before, there is no end to the amount of knowledge you can gain on the subject of Shameless Self-Promotion for yourself. The key is to start with a very good foundation and find out what works for you and know that you have to actually do something to have those sales regardless of how you are published.

If you are planning on doing series or multi-book writing. I recommend that you publish your first book, then get to work on the next immediately! If you are going to publish several books, you want to wait until at least book three to do a big push as far as marketing goes. You will find you make more money advertising/talking about book three (as they will then buy books one and two) than if you do book one, book two and book three. You will basically cut your effort into a third and make three times the profit. Plus, you hook them into wanting more.

You will find that all of these things become muscle memory. You just need to practice and you will find it gets easier as time goes on.

So are you ready?

I believe in you. You are amazing. Now . . . make it happen!

Top Ten Countdown to Shameless Self-Promotion

10. Get your website and socials as soon as possible. The name for your website and socials should be the same whenever you can.

9. Send newsletters. Twenty percent of your newsletter following will buy your next book.

8. Have your business card for you as an author at all times and give them out whenever possible.

7. Nail down your elevator pitch for you as an author and for every book/series you have. You should be able to say each in under fifteen seconds.

6. Don't spend a bunch of money on marketing materials. Invest time into connections instead.

5. Put yourself out there.

4. Don't buy social media followers.

3. Ask for reviews from anyone who tells you they read your book. Reviews help boost ratings everywhere.

2. Get continuous work out into the world. It doesn't need to be a full book. A short story for an anthology or an article on the subject your book is about will work.

1. Do not be afraid to ask others for help. Reach out to other authors online or in person. We are a community and in this together.

Meet Erika Lance

Erika Lance is a writer of horror, suspense, Sci-fi, and a little fantasy. She has been many things in this life, but she is most proud of being a nerd before it was cool. Growing up in the '80s and '90s, she will tell you, finding another female D&D player was rare.

She is also the CEO of 4 Horsemen Publications, Inc., Accomplishing Innovations Press, and The Little Horsemen. She is the host of Drinking with Authors podcast and co-host of the Eerie Travels podcast.

Erika fell in love with horror while watching Elvira and Dr. Paul Bearer on Saturday afternoon TV and was hooked. She believes that life is an adventure and it is built on the things you do, the people you surround yourself with, and most of all, the things you create.

She loves to create worlds and stories, finding that not all stories have happy endings.

Website: https://erikalance.com and https://accomplishinginnovationpress.com/

On Being a Good Literary Citizen
Claire Fullerton

The literary community is comprised of passionate people. We're a soul collective wielding words as a communicative art that gives us ways to reach out and touch someone, tell our stories, and share our perspectives of the world. We are writers with voices who hope to be heard. We live in a culture devoted to language as a creative expression. What we writers have in common outweighs any differences, and we operate in a synergistic, give-and-take community.

Because we are lucky to exist in the milieu of our chosen profession, the fundamental question concerns being an asset to the literary community. To put it succinctly, how can we, as individual writers, contribute to a greater whole?

Paradoxically, I liken the literary community to both society at large and the nucleus of a family. In both spheres, writers have something to share and want to do so with proper comportment. We walk a fine line between art for art's sake and the business of book promotion: There's the necessity of making sure readers know our books exist and the hope that we get the word out with a measure of dignity and self-awareness. We shudder at grandstanding but are eager to share our stories. We want to post on social media about our book-related achievements and appearances, but we don't want to overstay our welcome. It's a common dilemma to which all writers can relate.

The one thing we know is nobody with a book in the world operates alone. Authors count on each other, support each other, and recognize the aiding and abetting nature of a club in which we're thrilled to be a member. We are all nice people, with the social skills to prove it. We are like pack animals within a literary system, and we watch ourselves and each other to remain sensitive to the guidelines.

I consider the literary community tantamount to the hub of a wheel whose spokes keep it spinning in perpetual motion. The hub is comprised of a fraternity of authors and book promoters that share a mission, and the spokes represent supportive avenues to use with regard to a book's promotion. Neither entity is one without the other. We do well to bear in mind that the rules we apply to being a good literary citizen are the very same as those that apply to good manners.

I am naming some of the avenues available to authors as a case in point, in an effort to show how you can contribute to the writing community as a good literary citizen:

Book Blogs

Book bloggers are dedicated readers. Many bloggers are also authors, and the time and attention they give to providing a forum for book visibility are priceless for an author. Most book bloggers have a devoted audience. When your book is featured on their site, it leads to invaluable exposure.

Typically, a feature on a book blog includes a book's cover, description, author's bio, author's headshot, buy links, and sometimes, an author interview. Before authors query a book blogger, it's imperative that they follow the blog and engage, lest they seem like an opportunist. The steps to take in introducing yourself and your book to a book blogger are this:

Pitching: Write to the book blogger three months before your book's release date and tell them why you are enthusiastic about having your book featured on their blog. Make it plain you're familiar with the blog. Provide your book cover, description, and author bio. Conduct yourself respectfully in your full submission. Ask if there's anything else they'd like you to send.

Prior to feature: When you're featured on a book blog, share the blog's link on all of your social media outlets. This directs attention to the blogger's site and is part of a give-and-take dynamic where both parties are served.

After feature: After your book is featured, thank the blogger in a well-composed email, or go the extra step by delivering a handwritten note via mail. If you had bookmarks made to promote your book, include one with your handwritten note. Don't disappear from the blogger's life after your book is featured. Continue to engage with their site, in a show of support.

Facebook Book Groups

The book groups on Facebook are run by dedicated, organized book lovers. They offer authors the chance to introduce themselves and their book to the group's followers. Facebook book group moderators throw online parties where single and multiple author giveaways are featured. Most offer an author "takeover" day, where an author can post throughout the day about their book and engage with readers.

Some moderators interview authors by using Facebook Live. Many encourage authors to post fun facts about themselves and their writing process. Facebook book groups are a wonderful place for an author to post their book trailer. The book group pages are fun and dynamic. You can be a good literary citizen who shows appreciation to the moderator by doing the following:

- Join the book group page and engage with events, whether you do this in the moment or after the event is over.
- Send out an invitation to your book-loving friends to join the page.
- Help promote future events by sharing the book group's link on your social media outlets.
- If you're not in the habit of giving away your book, offer to contribute to an event by giving away bookmarks, or whatever swag you feel is appropriate.
- Support other authors during their book group events; comment on or like one of their posts. No gesture is too small.
- Keep your good manners on another author's post by refraining from mentioning your own book title or event.
- Thank the book page moderator for their hard work and express your gratitude for being included.

Podcasters

A podcast is a digital program made available over the internet or for download. There are many podcasts dedicated to authors and readers, and you can find them by conducting an online search. Podcasts attract consistent listeners. You can introduce yourself to a podcaster and submit as a potential guest by doing this:

Pitching: Craft your pitch by introducing yourself, including your bio, book title, book genre, and book description. Tell the podcaster you're an avid listener of their show. Detail precisely how you're a good fit for their audience. Include your book trailer and social media links. As in all submissions, provide ample lead time—three to four months is the standard. Follow up after four to six weeks with another email and be patient while waiting for a reply.

Show preparation: Once you're booked, mark your scheduled appearance on your calendar. The week before your guest appearance, share the date and time on your social media outlets. Prepare your environment by ensuring there will be no background noise or distractions. Consider using headphones, turning off your cell phone, settling your pets in another room, and having a glass of water at the ready.

During the show: Follow the podcaster's lead by being a good listener. Stay on point and answer all questions fully. The key to being a good guest is to do your part in making the show conversational, i.e., don't put the podcaster in the position of having to "pull teeth." Bring your personality to the table.

Follow up: Share the link to your podcast on social media, after it is given to you, and tag the podcaster. Thank the podcaster for having you on their show via email or handwritten note via mail.

Bookstores

The joy of a bookstore event comes from the author/reader connection. Audience members enjoy a name with a face, and in-store events are a delightful way for authors to meet readers. At bookstore events, authors read from their work, give a prepared speech, sign books, or are interviewed, according to the bookstore's preference. To be a good literary citizen, an author approaches a bookstore event with the same manners they'd display when visiting a friend at their house.

Pitching: Contact the bookstore's manager either by email or in person and express your enthusiasm for an event with respect to their schedule. Follow the bookstore's guidelines for submission in a timely manner. Typically, this involves filling out the bookstore's form that clearly defines the agreement between the author and the bookstore. Send a copy of your book to the bookstore manager and the owner. Once scheduled, promote your bookstore event on social media and tag the bookstore.

At the event: Arrive early to the event, and bring bookmarks and swag. Be prepared to speak comprehensively about your book, and be available to answer all questions. Stay at the event until the last book is signed.

Follow up: Thank the bookstore owner and manager, and follow up with an email or handwritten note.

Asking for an Endorsement of Your Book from Fellow Authors in the Literary Community

An author's endorsement of your book tells readers your book has been vetted and approved by another author. The more well-known the author, the better. It can be daunting for an author to ask for a book endorsement, but here are guidelines to make the request appealing and hopefully accepted:

Prior to pitching: Be sure to ask for an endorsement from an author that writes in your book's genre. Fundamentally, you are hoping to attract the attention of their readership. It should be a compatible fit. Take the time to read a book by the author whose endorsement you seek. To not do so is bad manners. Follow and engage on social media with the author and share his/her posts. If you have a blog, feature the author's work in a blog post. Sign up for the author's newsletter. Follow the author on Goodreads and BookBub.

Pitching: Write to the author and specifically tell them why you hope to receive their endorsement. Make it plain you're familiar with their work. Give the author at least two months to read the ARC of your book. Three months is better. State your deadline clearly.

Follow up: Once you receive their endorsement, and your book is out, mail the author an autographed copy of your book. If you have once asked an author for their endorsement, resist returning to them with your next book. A suggested option as a gesture of gratitude: Send a donation to your favorite library or literary center in the name of the author who endorsed your book. Continue to support the author who endorsed your book.

Giving Your Endorsement of a Fellow Author's Book

At some point, you will be asked to read and write an endorsement for a fellow author's book. It is an honor to be asked, and if you accept the assignment, keep your word. Here are guidelines for writing a book endorsement:

- Ask for the deadline date of your endorsement and commit to meeting it.
- Aim for two to three impactful sentences in your endorsement.
- Include the book's genre.
- Try to capture the overall spirit of the story.
- Fitting descriptive adjectives are useful.
- Keep your endorsement tense active.
- Prepare a succinct review, beyond your endorsement, to post on Goodreads and BookBub.
- Decide how you'd like your name to appear on the endorsement. It's appropriate to call yourself an author and mention one of your book titles.

Supporting Fellow Authors in the Literary Community on Your Blog

Again, the literary community is a give-and-take arena. Authors rarely forget who has supported their work, and it's always a pleasure to return the favor. It's nice to comment on and share your fellow author's social media posts and very effective to share a bit about their book on your blog. It communicates to your followers that you are an avid reader and a member of a literary community. Consider crafting a book post championing your fellow author's book with these guidelines:

- Title your blog post with the book title and author's name.
- At the top of the blog post, share the book cover.
- Add the book's description.
- If you've written a book review, include it. (Be sure to post that review online on Goodreads, BookBub, and book outlets, such as Amazon and Barnes and Noble.)
- Include the author's headshot or go to their website and copy and paste a creative photograph of them that will catch readers' attention.
- Include the author's bio, website, and social media links.
- Include the book's buy links.
- Share the blog post on your social media pages and be sure to tag the author.

Social Media Etiquette in the Literary Community

Most authors have an idea about how they want to appear on social media, the nature of their social media focus, and how much of their personal life they are willing to share. The task for an author using social media to promote their books is to balance the news of their book with how they want to be represented on social media as a person. It's advisable for an author to share a bit about their life, but it's wise to be judicious.

Some authors delineate their personal and professional lives on Facebook and Instagram by dedicating a business/author page exclusively for their books. It's an individual choice. There can be pitfalls in combining book promotion and your personal life, so the more mindful an author can be going into it, the better their appearance on social media. The idea is to not overdo it by posting too frequently. If an author over-does it on social media, they run the risk of viewers' eyes glazing over from too many posts. Over-posting can be counterproductive.

Here are some social media guidelines for an author to consider on their posts, as well as when they comment on others' posts.

- Consider your use of social media. Are you on social media to contribute interesting content to the community or are you on social media solely for the purpose of selling books? Try to strike a healthy balance.
- Decide how often to post about a book, pre-release. Posts can be used as teasers that become more frequent, once a book is available online for preorder.
- Decide how often to post about a book, its reviews, or your author interviews and appearances once your book is released. Posting every day is not necessary once your followers know you have a book in the world.
- An introductory caption for a post regarding a book review you've written should be short and sweet. It's good manners for an author to keep themselves out of the post's introduction, as well as out of the book review itself, so the focus is on the book that's been reviewed.
- It's nice to like and comment on other authors' posts when they post about their books, but maintain good manners by not mentioning your own books or any scheduled future appearances on another author's thread.
- Consider the polarizing dynamic of posting your political views on social media. There's a good chance

some followers will disagree, which could result in a negative impact.
- If you have endorsed another author's book and want to post about that book on social media, consider whether it's necessary to mention that your endorsement appears in that book. If you choose to mention your own endorsement of the book in your post, employ skillful word choice. Announcing that your endorsement is in the book runs the risk of the post being about you, as opposed to the book.
- Consider your boundaries and comfort zone with regard to how personal you want to be with your followers on social media. As an author, you are a public figure sharing your work, and using the forum to air certain aspects of your life with followers should be fully considered. Do you want to share nice photographs of where you live, your family, your pets, and your book recommendations, or do you want to post about your life's disappointments and personal struggles? What you post on social media tells your followers who you are, and it's best to be mindful.

The key to being a good citizen of the literary community is to conduct yourself as a team player while maintaining a good dose of grace and humility. Follow submission guidelines, show your gratitude to those who support your work, and repay the favor in kind.

Top Ten Countdown to Asking for a Book Endorsement

10. Ask for an endorsement from an author that writes in your book's genre.

9. Read a book by the author whose endorsement you seek.

8. Follow and engage on social media with the author.

7. Share his/her posts.

6. If you have a blog, feature the author's work in a blog post.

5. Sign up for the author's newsletter.

4. Follow the author on Goodreads and BookBub.

3. Write to the author and specifically tell them why you hope to receive their endorsement.

2. Give the author two to three months to read the ARC of your book and include your deadline.

1. Show your gratitude to the author by sending an email, handwritten note, or donation to a literary community in their name.

Meet Claire Fullerton

Claire Fullerton is the multiple award-winning author of four novels and one novella. A contributor to numerous anthologies and literary magazines, she lives in Malibu, California, with her husband and three German shepherds. Claire is an avid student of Shakespeare for the stage. She is represented by Julie Gwinn of the Seymour Literary Agency.

Website: https://www.clairefullerton.com

What Every Author Should Know About Building Their Website
Natalie Obando

Authors who are just beginning their writing journey often think that the only thing they need to concern themselves with is their book and completing it. And while that might be partially true, from what I have learned in nearly two decades working with authors is that you must have an online presence to truly succeed as an author. Specifically, you need a website. And even seasoned authors often find out later, after many redesigns, just exactly what is needed for their book to succeed.

In my work with the Authentic Voices Fellowship, a program I founded and chair through Women of Color Writers and Women's National Book Association for marginalized voices, we teach not only craft but also discuss key elements for successful authors. In this fellowship, our fellows take home the most important staple skills and systems an author must have in place prior to the release of their book, and most often, prior to even pitching their manuscript to an agent. One of these skills is website development.

Having a website today serves many purposes. For authors, having a website is as important as having an email address. A website is absolutely essential to your ability to communicate as an author to potential readers, editors, media, and buyers. A website is a platform for visibility and sales. Like any business today, your success as an author strongly relies on how readily available you and your product are to potential customers. The easier you can be discovered, the more potential customers you have. Your website is your first step in marketing yourself and your work and creating discoverability.

An author website is a little different than other business websites. As an author, make no mistake, you ARE a business. You produce a product that you need to sell, and hopefully, as you continue to write and create more books, you are selling more products (books). You and your books are your products. You are selling yourself (your expertise, your story) to editors, agents, and media, and you are selling your book to readers. Luckily for the inexperienced, you don't have to be a website designer. You need only know the basics when it comes to content (at first). As you become more and more familiar with the process of creating and working with your site, you can add more. All you need to know at the start is what you want your site to look like and have a couple of sites to use as references.

Before you start building your website, make sure that you purchase your name as a domain. This is extremely important because there are people who make livings buying semi-famous names or names that trickle into the media and then sell them to others at a higher cost. Domain name brokers make a lot of money selling your name right back to you, so make sure to secure that first. If you are thinking about using your book name as a domain, keep in mind that if you plan on writing future books, the name of one book might not be the best option. I always suggest that my authors not only buy their books' domain names, but their own names as well. Every domain that you purchase can be redirected to your primary site.

While creating a website can seem daunting at first, with today's easy-to-use technology, it is as simple as using a template and replacing its content with your own. Let's discuss what your website should have in terms of content.

An author's website should consist of the following pages or anchored sections: a home or landing page, an about the author page, a book/s page, a contact page, and a media page (one that is visible and one that is hidden) and a blog page (this will later help you generate search engine optimization, SEO). I prefer separate pages for each with an easy-to-view page menu bar across the top. This allows the viewer to click on each menu tab and be redirected to the page of their choice. However, there are others who prefer to have one flowing page of information with each menu tab to be redirected to a section on the same page. It is redirected to that portion by setting up an "anchor" on the section so that the menu tab redirects to that section on the same page. Both versions are fine and the style is completely up to the author.

Other elements to include on your website are email captures and opt-ins and social media widgets and links. If you are further along in your career, perhaps an events page.

Let's take a deeper look into each of the pages and sections authors need on their site.

Home/Landing Page

This page or section should give an overview of you, your brand, and your work (book/s). It should have things available at a quick glance and make the viewer want to stay for more. It's a great place to put your mission statement as a writer or an overview of what you write. If you have any endorsements from other writers, writing instructors, writing mentors, or colleagues, you can put these here, as well. The general idea is to make sure that this isn't too bogged down with a lot of information and allows the visitor to get the best glance of you and all your work as quickly and easily as possible. Think of it as a visible and constantly active pitch to readers, agents, and the media. It is the first thing that a visitor sees. What do you want that at-a-glance pitch to say about you? Make sure that your landing page is not all text and that it is visually appealing as well. Use an image (or a few) here that captures your brand and book/s. It doesn't have to be a picture of you and your book, but the image should echo the story that you are telling in your writing in a more visual sense.

About the Author Page

This page or section should give the reader a more in-depth view of you. It should be a well-crafted, longer bio that tells the reader all the reasons you write what you do and how you do it. Who are you influenced by? Where did you grow up? Where do you live? Do you have any awards or mentions? On this page, think of incorporating what makes you relatable to the reader and what might make the reader connect to you on a personal level. I tend to like to write and see these in a first-person format because they feel like the authors are talking directly to the readers. However, I lean toward the more casual and approachable style of connecting with readers because that's my personality type and my brand. If you are going for a more literary and professional tone, a bio in third person might be best suited for you. This can be as long as you would like it to be, but try not to be too overindulgent. A great author headshot works well here. If you have any professional lifestyle photos, use them here as well. It's always great to see authors in action via the stories the images on their website tell. Please remember that photos on your site should be more curated than photos on your social media. Since your site is searchable and public, make sure that what you are showcasing is tastefully chosen to represent you.

A side note on photos:

If you look at websites that you like, chances are that they have clean and crisp images. These images likely came from a professional photographer or a camera that took photos with great quality and resolution. Old cell phone photos simply won't cut it when it comes to making sure that your site looks great. In fact, most visually appealing sites are appealing because of the photos. This is why I always recommend hiring a professional photographer with professional camera equipment and an understanding of lighting. There are many professional photographers all around the world but the service that I love to use with my clients and for myself is Flytographer. Flytographer is a company that has a vetted and curated list of fairly priced professional photographers around the world whose work you can review prior to booking. I've used this company for photos across the world, and they are great! What's great about using this company is that if you ever have a trip that you want to showcase on your site for some lifestyle photos, you'll likely be able to find a top-quality photographer who can also give professional direction for lifestyle images that will look great on a site.

Book Page

Assuming that you have a book, this is where you would not only highlight it but also make sure to sell it. Your book page should have a synopsis of the book, typically what's on the back cover and a bit more, as well as the book's metadata (i.e. ISBN, publisher, release date, page count). The book page should have all the different purchase links to your book. If you have any reviews of your book, make sure to highlight a few of the best here in case a reader wants a bit more credibility before they purchase your book. There are a lot of fun things that I've been seeing authors include on their book pages like playlists, book club kits, and book trailers.

Contact Page

All websites need a method to get in contact with the author. My suggestion is NEVER to put your personal email address, address, or phone number onto your website. Spammers and scammers are more abundant than ever, and making your contact information public makes you more susceptible to them. Use a contact form on your contact page that has a spam and bot filter. The more levels of protection that you have over your contact information, the better you protect yourself from potential cyber-attacks.

Media Pages

Two different media pages should serve two different functions. The first media page we'll discuss is the one that is visible and has its own tab on the menu bar. This page is one that helps to create and elevate your credibility as a writer by highlighting reviews, interviews, podcasts, and any other media highlights that showcase and praise your work. This page also helps to showcase your ability to work with the media and how you interview. Feel free to use reviews from Goodreads and Amazon here too.

The second media page, the hidden page, should only be accessible by a link that you give to actual media contacts. This page serves as a tool to make the life of media contacts easier, so it should have all the items they might need when providing coverage about you and your book. Pages that I build typically have a downloadable media kit, both short and long bios, author headshots in both web resolution and high resolution, images of your book cover in both web resolution and high resolution, and full URL links to your social media. These are all the things that many media workers will request from you that also may be too large to email (large pictures) or may be needed ASAP and you might be too busy to answer an email. Giving this link to media contacts once they have initiated contact is a good way to let them know that you are easy to work with, appreciate their coverage, are trying to make their life easier, and that you know what you're doing. I always make sure that this page is hidden so that spammers do not get a hold of any contact information that might be on this page.

Blog Page

I am a HUGE proponent and fan of author blog pages. Aside from all the benefits of what a well-written and strategic blog can do for your SEO, this is a place to really show off your writing skills. It's a place for readers to explore your writing with little effort from the reader. If you can write an entertaining and informative blog post, chances are potential readers will judge your book by your blog and pick up a copy. I like to look at a blog like a net that can capture your blog readers and transfer them into paying readers.

Keep your blog current. Trending with topics in the media helps drive traffic to your site. As an author, the best thing to blog about is other people's books. This not only helps you uplift other authors, but the highlighted authors will help spread awareness of your platform.

Email Capture

You've seen it on every site, that (sometimes pesky) little box that pops up asking for your email right when the site comes up. This email capture box, sometimes called a lightbox popup, is something that a site visitor will have to engage with in order to proceed. They either have to close it or fill it out in order to proceed. It is an author's best tool for sales and any other call to action. According to MightyForms, an industry leader in this area, pop-ups make up more than 66% of all enabled email capture forms. This means that the subscribe button on the bottom of your website simply won't cut it. Typically, these pop-up boxes provide value to the site visitor. For instance, a discount or promo code might be received if they add their email. Or perhaps you might give them access to exclusive content. On either occasion, this opt-in method allows the site visitor to become more of an insider into your world. This opting-in is letting you know that they are interested. Your website is a great place to capture email addresses and contact information. The more email addresses that you have, the more potential customers/ readers you can reach out to directly.

Make sure to add an email capture pop-up box on your landing or home page.

Social Media Widgets and Links

As many authors know, social media is a way to communicate directly with your fans. And while not every social media platform may be for every author, it is important that you choose the social media platform that you find easy to engage with and that suits your audience. Since you are taking the time to engage on social media, make sure that your website directs its visitor back to social media platforms. Because links on the site might get lost, you want to make sure to place social media widgets at the very top and bottom of the website so that they are easy to see and/or go back to and find. Make sure that these links, as well as any other links on your site, open in a separate tab so as not to direct visitors away from your site.

Events Page

Once you get to the point where you are involved in author events, an events page is a must. It is a great way to allow your readers to keep in contact with you and make yourself accessible to connect with them live. Whether joining group readings, panels, bookstore signings, or open mics, it's great for visitors to know where and how they can support you in person or online.

Some Final Notes on Your Website

Your website is the largest and most trusted platform that you have as an author. It's the first place your audience or prospective agent and publisher will turn to when they want to know more about you. It isn't influenced by social media algorithms, and it is a great base to funnel sales through. Your website makes your work searchable. It should be your hub of online activity. Your online presence or lack of it can tremendously influence your success as an author.

When it comes to the aesthetics of the website, while the design is definitely a reflection of the author, try to keep it clean and easy to read. It may be very tempting to get overly flowery with it, but the best practice is to keep it visually appealing and easy on the eyes. This helps keep it simple for maintenance too.

Don't be afraid to try to build a website. It's okay to make mistakes. Just remember to keep saving as you go along and have fun!

Top Ten Countdown to Designing an Author Website

10. Take a look at the websites of other authors who have books similar to yours and have a career path similar to what you are aiming for. Take note of how they make their website flow. How do they make their work stand out? What works? What doesn't? Use these sites as a reference when building yours.

9. Buy both your name as a domain and your book title or series as a domain. You can redirect either to the site. If you have to choose one, choose your name.

8. You don't need to be a web designer to build a site. There are many host platforms that have hundreds of beautiful design templates. I recommend WIX.

7. Set up an email capture directly on your website. I recommend two, one that stays in place on the site at all times and one that pops up and that must be closed out by the site visitor.

6. Make sure to have the following pages or anchored sections—Landing, About the Author, About the Book, and Blog. Add a media page when the reviews and interviews start rolling in about your book so that your site showcases your book and/or writing credibility as well.

5. Have several places to purchase your book on your website. Don't forget to make preorders available as well.

4. Connect all of your active social media to your site via links and widgets.

3. Don't forget to blog! This is a great way to connect to the writing community and also generate SEO.

2. Have a hidden page for media assets for media professionals that have the following items: web and high-resolution author photos and book cover photos, a media kit as downloadable PDF, an author Q&A, and bios, short (120 words or fewer) and long.

1. Above all else, make sure that your site is a reflection of who you are and what's important to you. It's your space in the online world to customize and showcase your authentic self.

Meet Natalie Obando

For nearly two decades Natalie Obando has worked in the world of books as the founder of Do Good Public Relations Group and the grassroots organization, Women of Color Writers Podcast and Programming. She is the current national president of the 105-year-old non-profit, the Women's National Book Association (WNBA), overseeing all chapters across the nation. She is the founder and chair of Authentic Voices—a four-month-long program that immerses people from marginalized communities in writing, editing, marketing, and publishing. Natalie has been a speaker at literary conferences across the United States helping authors and publishers promote their work and drive equity in publishing.

Website: https://dogoodprgroup.com

SOCIAL Media
Meredith R. Stoddard

Imagine a big party. People are milling around in groups usually based on their shared interests. Then you, the writer, walk in. Your dress shoes are already pinching. You try to unobtrusively smooth down the slightly rumpled dress or sport coat that you fished out of the back of your closet when you heard this was a party you shouldn't miss. You look around and wonder how you can work the room to sell your books.

These days social media is the party you shouldn't miss. It is essential for an author to have a presence on social media. In a time where millions of books are available, discoverability becomes more important by the day. But many authors don't know where to begin, which social media platforms they should focus on, or what content will be most effective. The most important tip I can give about using social media to promote your books is to lean in to the social part.

In this chapter, we'll talk about ways that you can:

- Focus on the best platforms for your audience
- Target readers
- Maintain engagement

Understanding Algorithms

You can think of the algorithm as the party's host introducing you to the people it thinks you will enjoy meeting. It's the program that determines which users it shows your posts to and how it prioritizes the posts it shows.

Because companies adjust their algorithms all the time, it's hard to explain what posts work best for each platform. They also tailor their algorithm for their unique user base. The common trait is that most algorithms favor engagement. No matter which platform you are on, the more comments, likes, and reshares a post gets, the more people the algorithm will show it to.

It's important to keep the business model of social media platforms in mind. While each company varies, social media companies make their money in two main ways:

- By collecting demographic data on its users and selling that data
- By selling advertisements on its platform

The more time users spend on their platform, the more data they collect, and the more people see and click on their ads. The algorithm is what feeds each user the posts most likely to keep them engaged for the longest amount of time and to keep them coming back.

For authors and other small business owners, that means we want to make posts that are as engaging as possible. Here are some examples.

- Posts that pose questions are effective in getting comments. This or that? Would you rather? Or asking opinions on topics related to your books.
- Easy to read and understand memes (humorous images, videos, or text that are shared on social media) are good for getting responses as well.
- Images. People often skim through social media, so images will get more attention than words alone. Try to include an image with your posts (unless it's a video-sharing platform).

You should also follow up on those posts. Respond to comments that you get. Keep the conversation going, and it will improve your post's reach.

Where to Post

Which social media platforms you focus your efforts on will depend on where your target readers are and what kind of content you are comfortable creating and posting. Let's take a look at the top platforms and how you can use them.

Facebook

With 2.91 billion visitors a month, Facebook is the biggest party in town. You will likely want to have a presence on Facebook.

While Facebook is huge with both marketers and consumers, its growth rate has slowed considerably in the last couple of years. Likewise, the amount of time the average user spends on it per day is also shrinking from 38 minutes to 33 minutes. Where Facebook can benefit authors is through the ability to target potential readers both through how authors use the community and through targeted ads.

Ways you can use Facebook

You may already have a personal profile on Facebook. For your author business, you should make a business Page as well. Pages are used by businesses to promote themselves and share information about their products and services. It also lets you unlock features in Facebook like the Meta Business Suite which schedules posts on Facebook and Instagram and the Ad Center where you can manage Facebook Ads. Unfortunately, Facebook's algorithm doesn't promote your Page posts within users' feeds. This is because Facebook wants to drive Page owners to pay for advertising. If you want to target and build connections on Facebook without paid promotions, Facebook Groups should be your focus. Groups can be started by anyone with similar interests. The Group administrators will set rules and invite people to join, or people can search for groups related to their interests and join. There are Facebook Groups for books, genres, specific series fans, author fan groups, and more. Authors utilize Groups in two main ways. First, you can start your own reader group. This is especially good if you have more than one book. Your reader group will help you connect with your readers about future books and promote books in your back catalog. An engaged reader group can be a great resource for staying connected with your fans and, ultimately, sell more books.

You can also use Groups to find new readers. Search for fan groups of your genre, of authors whose books and voices are like yours, or of your favorite authors. If you find people who like the same books that you do, chances are they might like your books too. If you are writing nonfiction, find Groups that are interested in the topic you're writing about. Remember when you join a new group, read the rules. Group administrators usually have rules about self-promotion, such as when and how it can be done. The group may have a particular thread or allow promotions on a particular day. Don't violate these rules. Instead of spamming groups with information about your book, focus on connecting with the users in the group about your shared interests. Then use whatever promotional occasions arise or wait for it to come up organically.

Twitter

Twitter is a different party than Facebook. It is more fast-paced and free-wheeling. Posts are limited to 280 characters, so being succinct is essential. With 211 million daily active users, there is a lot of potential for connection on Twitter.

Like Facebook, Twitter has a lot of users, but its growth rate is slowing. When you add the turmoil of changing ownership and going private, that growth may slow even more. However, there can still be a lot of benefits for writers and authors on Twitter. A robust and active writing community means that it can be a great place to connect with other writers, industry professionals, journalists, and readers.

Who to Follow

Making the most of Twitter begins with following the people whose tweets you want to see and who you want to see your tweets. Search Twitter for readers who are talking about books comparable to yours. If there are authors in your genre who are popular, then you can follow the accounts that follow those authors. When you follow someone, they will often follow you in return. This way you can attract readers who will likely be interested in your book. Then make sure your content is engaging for them.

Once you find some accounts of your target readers, check their tweets on Fridays for the #FollowFriday hashtag. People use this hashtag on Fridays to endorse accounts that they like. This can help expand your network.

Hashtags

The volume of posts on Twitter can be staggering. Hashtags are a tool for finding and following discussions on Twitter. People use hashtags to link related tweets. Searching for a hashtag will bring up tweets containing that hashtag, allowing you to follow the conversation more easily. Here are some hashtags that are useful for writers.

#WritingCommunity
#WritersLift
#AmWriting
#AmWriting(insert genre)
#FridayReads
#WriterWednesday
#BookGiveaway

Twitter events

Another way to connect on Twitter is to look for events that relate to your book or themes within your book. These can be holidays, awareness events, and even scheduled events on Twitter. For example, I write folklore-inspired fiction. The hashtag #FolkloreThursday highlights a conversation around a weekly folklore theme. I use that prompt to join the conversation and to find other folklore enthusiasts to follow. If you write books similar to a television show, such as Regency Era romance, then the premier of Bridgerton would be a great event to tweet using #Bridgerton.

If you want to connect with other writers, events like NaNoWriMo (National Novel Writing Month) and Camp NaNoWriMo offer opportunities to join the conversation.

Instagram

If Twitter is like a rave, Instagram is afternoon tea in a pretty garden. With 2 billion active monthly users, it's a great way to reach readers. Originally a photo-sharing app, Instagram has long been known for image curation and aesthetics. However, influence from other social networks is changing attitudes on Instagram. In 2021, Instagram shifted its focus to video sharing by changing its algorithm to promote reels, short videos under ninety seconds, rather than photos. Because of this shift, many users repurpose their short video content across Instagram, TikTok, and YouTube Shorts.

Instagram is owned by Meta, the same parent company as Facebook. Like Facebook, Instagram's growth rate is slowing, though not as quickly. Instagram offers many opportunities to connect with readers and writers.

Who to Follow

Who you follow on Instagram is similar to who you should follow on Twitter. Look for other authors in your genre, hashtags related to your genre, and themes in your book. Follow those accounts, and they will likely follow you back. As you are building your account, Instagram will also suggest accounts for you to follow. For example, if you are just starting to build a following, you should stick to following accounts related to books and your genre. This way, the algorithm will make better suggestions for you.

One unique thing about Instagram is that you can follow hashtags. If you write fantasy romance or science fiction, you can follow #fantasyromance or #scifi to keep up to date on trends within your genre. This will also help you find new accounts to follow. A hashtag that you should definitely follow is #bookstagram.

#Bookstagram

Many book reviewers have accounts on Instagram where they will post reviews. These are the accounts that you will want to follow and cultivate relationships with. Their posts are usually marked with #bookstagram. Authors and publishers frequently send Advanced Review Copies to bookstagrammers. Each bookstagrammer has their own niche, so start by looking for reviewers who will likely fit your genre.

Types of Content

Instagram posts come in several different types.

- **Photos** are static photos or graphics. You can also make multi-photo posts called carousels.
- **Reels** are short videos of ninety seconds or fewer. They are frequently humorous and set to music. Reels can be made within the Instagram app using its Reels editor.
- **Livestreams** are another option. This enables you to broadcast to your followers or connect with other accounts for live discussions. After your livestream is over, you can post the video to your feed.

- **Stories** are messages that are pushed to your followers. When you post a story, Instagram will notify your followers of it. This is great for announcing news because it depends less on the algorithm.

TikTok

If you've been to a Barnes & Noble recently, you've probably seen a table labeled #BookTok Favorites. With a billion monthly users, TikTok is becoming an increasingly prominent force in marketing books, especially in genres that appeal to younger readers such as young adult, fantasy, romance, and science fiction. That is all thanks to the #BookTok community of readers, reviewers, and authors.

TikTok exploded during the pandemic and continues to be one of the fastest-growing platforms. It invites users to post videos anywhere from seven seconds to three minutes. And gives users the tools to make and edit those videos. Users can decide if videos are viewable by anyone or only by their followers. Where Instagram is known for curated aesthetics, TikTok is all about authenticity. Many videos are simply users talking to the camera about whatever they're thinking.

For You Page

Unlike most other platforms, TikTok lets users choose to view a feed made up of only those accounts that they follow or take their chances on the "For You Page." This is a feed that TikTok compiles based on your likes and follows as well as the amount of time you spend watching certain videos. TikTok's big strength is in the algorithm it uses to determine what videos it shows each user on their For You Page. It is very good at delivering targeted content for users' interests. This targeting means that the people who see your videos are as likely to be new to your content as they are to be your existing followers, making it easy to build a following on TikTok, if you post consistently.

Types of Content

- **Videos**, as stated, can be anywhere from seven seconds to three minutes. TikTok also allows users to duet (allows you to add your commentary side-by-side with another's video) or stitch (when you incorporate clips of other people's videos in your own) other users' videos to respond to them.
- **Follower only videos** are videos addressed just to the users who follow you. This is great for strengthening relationships with your followers.
- **Livestreams** can be used to connect with other users and to attract new followers. Authors and BookTokers frequently use livestreams to discuss books and trends in publishing.
- **"Now"** is a feature on TikTok that allows users to connect with their friends in the moment. When one of your friends posts a Now, you are invited to share a short video or photo of what you are doing at that moment. This feature is designed to deepen connections between users.

Pinterest

With 431 million active users per month, Pinterest is a platform that shouldn't be underestimated. Pinterest also has an affluent user base, with 45% of users having a household income of $100,000 or more. Let's talk about how you can market your books to these users.

If you're unfamiliar with Pinterest, it's easiest to think about it as a virtual corkboard where you can "pin" images or videos you find in magazines, newspapers, or online. Those images usually include links to articles, blog posts, or products for sale. Users can make a pin board about any subject that doesn't violate the terms of use. Users who have similar interests can "follow" other users' boards or search for items or topics to find things to pin to their own boards.

For authors, Pinterest boards are a great way of collecting and organizing your research, or mood and aesthetics while researching and writing. If you want to keep that information private, you can make your board "Secret" to prevent other users from seeing it. If you want to share this information once your book is released, you can change the setting to make it public. This provides your readers with a behind-the-scenes peek at your research and mood for a book.

When a board is public, you can regularly post to it and invite your readers or potential readers to follow it. You can make public boards for each book to post book quotes, covers, promotional graphics, and related articles. Boards for your genre or tropes within your book would also be a good idea. As with other social media sites, your visibility on Pinterest depends on an algorithm, and the algorithm favors engagement and fresh content. Post visually engaging content on a consistent basis. Engagement on Pinterest is measured by how many people re-pin, click on, or comment on your posts.

YouTube

While YouTube seems more like a content site than a social site. The ability of anyone to post and anyone to comment on videos makes it a social media platform. With two billion monthly active users, it should be a platform that you consider.

One benefit of posting to YouTube is that if users subscribe to your videos, they will be notified when you post a new one.

Booktube

Much like bookstagram and BookTok communities, YouTube has its own community of book reviewers. The platform allows for longer videos than TikTok or Instagram. However, the most popular BookTube videos on YouTube are short and pithy because of the influence of the shorter video platforms. YouTube also has its own short video platform, YouTube Shorts which can be accessed through the YouTube app on your smart phone. BookTube videos are not just reviews. Some BookTubers also post skits, interviews, and videos based on prompts by other BookTubers. Like other platforms, working with BookTubers starts by building relationships. Find some BookTubers who review books in your genre and begin by subscribing to them and commenting on their videos.

AuthorTube

If you're wondering what kinds of videos you should be posting as an author, search YouTube for "AuthorTube." If you want to start, there is an "AuthorTube Newbie Prompt" which gives you a list of questions to answer in an introductory video. After that, your content can include whatever you like. You can talk about your writing process, book reviews of your own, and more BookTube and AuthorTube prompts. You can also make videos about topics related to your book. Once again, relationship building will help you garner views. Subscribing and commenting on other authors' videos will help you start that process.

Top Social Platforms

Platform	TYPE OF CONTENT	TOP AGE DEMOGRAPHIC	GROWTH RATE IN 2021	GENDER RATIO (ONLY 2 GENDERS AVAILABLE)	POPULAR GENRES
FACEBOOK	• Text (including links) • Images • Videos • Livestream • Short Videos	25-34 (31.5%)	.8%	• 43% female • 57% male	All
TWITTER	• Text (including links) • Images • Videos • Spaces (Live Audio)	18-29 (42%)	.2%	• 38.4% female • 61.6% male	All
INSTAGRAM	• Images • Videos • Livestreams • Short Videos	25-34 (31.2%)	3.7%	• 48.4% female • 51.8% male	All
TIKTOK	• Short Videos • Livestreams	10-19 (25%)	18.3%	• 61% female • 39% male	Young Adult, Fantasy, Science Fiction, Romance, Erotica, Thriller, Mystery, General
PINTEREST	• Images (including links) • Videos	50-64 (38%) 30-49 (34%) 18-29 (-32%)	7.8%	• 78% female • 22% male	All fiction, Cookbooks, Craft books
YOUTUBE	• Videos • Short videos	15-35 (highest reach)	4.9%	• 46% female • 54% male	All

Social Networks for Book Lovers

Up to now, we've been looking at social media sites that don't have specific audiences. However, there are some social media sites that focus on books and reading. We're going to focus on two networks where readers can review books and follow authors, and where authors can connect with readers.

Goodreads

Goodreads has been around since 2007. It started as a Facebook-style social network for readers. Users set up their profiles including their Bookshelves of books that they have read and want to read. They also friend other users that they may know who like to read similar books. As users read books, they can review the book on its page. That review is then shown to their friends on the site through a feed similar to other social media feeds. Users can also follow authors on Goodreads and will be notified when those authors release new books and post to the site. Goodreads also has forums where readers and authors can discuss relevant topics.

With 125 million members and 50 million active monthly users, Goodreads can be an important component of your marketing plan. When a book is uploaded to Amazon, it is automatically also uploaded to Goodreads. As an author, you will want to claim your author page and your books. Once you have claimed your author page, you can link it with your blog so that Goodreads will automatically update your page when you post to your blog. Then you can encourage readers to follow you and review your books. All of this helps you build word of mouth among an active community of readers and book lovers. The forums are a great place to connect with new readers, as well.

One way to build a buzz for your book on Goodreads is to run a Giveaway. For a fee, Goodreads will host and promote your giveaway. They offer multiple packages with varying amounts of promotion. Depending on the package you purchase, Goodreads will promote your giveaway in users' feeds and send promotional emails to your followers. It will also send emails to the winners, reminding them to review your book.

BookBub

BookBub is not primarily a social media site. It is best known for its daily newsletters that feature free and marked down books curated for each subscriber according to their preferred genres. A BookBub Feature Deal for an author can be a huge marketing win. However, it can also be costly, and you must be selected based on some specific criteria. There is also a social aspect to BookBub's site that doesn't cost anything and will help you get the word out about your book.

Much like Goodreads, users can friend other users and post recommendations for the books that they like. Asking your readers who are on BookBub to do this can help build word of mouth. You can also invite your readers and potential readers to follow you. When a reader follows an author on BookBub, the site will send them an email to notify them that the author has a new release. You can also follow and recommend your favorite authors, or other authors in your genre. This can help you build a network of support. The more follows and recommendations you have on BookBub, the easier it will be to get one of those coveted Feature Deals when you apply.

It would be impossible to cover all social media sites in this chapter because there are new ones popping up all the time. Some others that you should consider, depending on your genre and demographic, are Tribel, Tumbler, Discord, Reddit, Snapchat, Twitch, LinkedIn, Lemon8, and WhatsApp. The social media landscape is constantly evolving. Pay attention to those shifts, and always seek out new opportunities and methods for connecting with potential readers.

What to Post

Imagine that you are standing, drink in hand, with a new group of people chatting about your love of books. As you're talking about your shared interest, another author walks up wearing a sandwich board and waving a copy of their book at anyone who glances their way. Everyone who encounters the sandwich board writer rolls their eyes.

This is the real-life equivalent of the spammer, a writer on social media who posts nothing but self-promotion. Spammers include links to their book listing, their Author Central page, or their Facebook Page in more than 20% of their posts. All they seem to say is "buy my book," "like my page," "follow me." Spammers get unfollowed quickly, or they are simply ignored.

Are there times when it's okay to post links to your books? Yes. Here are some examples of when you should self-promote.

- Running a sale or free promo
- Just got a great review
- Article in the media about you or your book
- Won an award
- Gave an interview
- Have an event like a book signing

All of these are good reasons to post about your book. Stick to the no more than 20% rule and you should be fine.

While spamming sales links is frowned upon, posting about your process for writing your book is not. Many readers are also aspiring authors, and even those who don't often appreciate being able to look behind the scenes at what goes into writing and publishing. This has the added benefit of building buzz about your book before it comes out. You can also release teasers for your work in progress as you write. I do this most Tuesdays using the hashtag #TeaserTuesday.

Another way to keep readers engaged without spamming them about your book is to post about related topics. Search on topics related to what you write, like your genre, subject matter, settings, and themes. I write books about a Gaelic-speaking folklorist in North Carolina. So, I have Google Alerts set for keywords related to my books, such as Scottish Gaelic, Scottish folklore, North Carolina folklore, Scotland, Celtic folklore, and so on. I get emails weekly that list articles related to those keywords, and I share those articles with my readers. This way I am sharing information related to my books, but not specifically about my books. I keep my readers interested in my book's theme or genre while continuing related conversations.

Another way to keep your readers engaged is by boosting authors who write books similar to yours. They might be in the same genre or about a similar subject. I don't know any reader who says, 'I only read books by this author.' Other authors are not competition. The more people read, the more they want to read. Sharing books by other authors helps your readers find things to read between your books, and it builds goodwill in the author community.

I've got one final word on what to post. Conventional wisdom says that polite conversation at social events should avoid hot-button topics like politics, religion, and money. Social media is a little more permissive when it comes to these subjects. There are plenty of folks out there who will tell you to avoid them. But writers are citizens too, and some of what we write might touch on these topics. It's up to you to decide whether you want to talk about these things on social media. You determine your own brand as a writer. Just be ready to deal with pushback when you get it. Arguments on social media are almost inevitable. You decide how you deal with them and how long you let them go on. While the algorithm favors engagement, that might not be the kind of engagement you want to encourage.

The simple prescription for posting on social media is to be yourself and behave as you would if you were face-to-face with people at a cocktail party. It's up to you to decide what topics you're comfortable with and what you're not. If you're a person who likes to talk about politics or religion or money, have at it, but realize you risk alienating potential readers who disagree with your opinions. The general rule is don't say anything that you would be embarrassed to say to a person's face or a group of people at a party.

Managing It All

With an ever-growing number of platforms, types of content, and ways to promote your books and connect with readers, you're probably asking yourself how you can possibly manage it all and still have time to write. Here are some strategies that you can use to help you post consistently and make the most of your time.

Banking Content: One of the keys to feeding the various algorithms is to post consistently. However, some days you just don't feel like making a video, or finding the right graphic, or writing a post. You can get ahead of this by taking a day or two every month to create videos, images, and posts that you can then spread over the next few weeks. This frees up your time during the rest of the month to work on writing.

Repurposing Content: There are several different types of content that you will likely be posting: videos, images, text posts, and links to articles your readers might find interesting. You can post each of these across several platforms. A video can be shared on TikTok, Instagram, and YouTube. An image can work for Instagram, Facebook, Twitter, and Pinterest. A link can be shared on Facebook, Twitter, and Pinterest, among others. Know what you can post where, and you will be able to repurpose content across multiple platforms.

REPURPOSE CONTENT ACROSS PLATFORMS

CONTENT TYPE	Facebook	Twitter	Instagram	TikTok	Pinterest	YouTube
TEXT (With Links)	✓	✓				
IMAGES	✓	✓	✓		✓ (with links)	
SHORT VIDEOS	✓	✓	✓	✓	✓	✓
VIDEOS (Longer than 90 seconds)	✓	✓	✓	✓ (Up to 3 minutes)	✓	✓
LIVESTREAMS	✓	✓	✓	✓		✓

(3rd Party Service required to Livestream to more than one platform at the same time.)

Scheduling Posts: Much like banking content, you can also schedule posts ahead of time for many platforms. Facebook Page (not your personal profile) and Instagram posts can be scheduled using the Meta Business Suite. Twitter has a free program called Tweetdeck that allows you to schedule your Tweets. You can also invest in a social media manager program, such as Hootsuite, SproutSocial, Buffer, and Later. These programs allow you to schedule content to multiple platforms at once and, in some cases, monitor the performance of posts across platforms. Some will even suggest articles that might interest your followers. Scheduling your posts at the beginning of the month or week can free up the rest of your time to focus on writing.

Conclusion

I hope this has given you a good overview of your social media options. Don't feel like you have to build a following on all of them at once. Choose the platforms that you think will be most effective for connecting with your readers and build each of them in stages. Focus on connecting with readers who are fans of your genre and authors who are similar to you. Engagement is key to building relationships on social media and getting the algorithms to work for you.

Sources

Brent Barnhart, "20 must-know Facebook stats for marketers in 2022" Sprout Social, March 8, 2022, https://sproutsocial.com/insights/facebook-stats-for-marketers/.

Brent Barnhart, "Social media demographics to inform your brand's strategy in 2022", Sprout Social, March 2, 2022, https://sproutsocial.com/insights/new-social-media-demographics/.

Brent Barnhart, "41 of the most important social media marketing statistics for 2022", Sprout Social, March 22, 2022, https://sproutsocial.com/insights/social-media-statistics/.

Craig Smith, "Goodreads Statistics and Facts (2022)", DMR, July 18, 2022, https://expandedramblings.com/index.php/goodreads-facts-and-statistics/.

L. Ceci, "Global YouTube user growth 2016-2021", Statista, Aug 23, 202, https://www.statista.com/statistics/805671/youtube-viewer-number-growth-world/.

Top Ten Countdown to Social Media Do's and Don'ts

10. DO focus on engaging with readers. Start conversations and engage with people. You never know who might be looking for their next great read.

9. DON'T feed trolls. Everyone on the internet has an opinion, and an easy way to voice it. There are some people who simply enjoy stirring conflict and getting reactions out of people. Responding to these trolls only encourages them to continue and sometimes escalate.

8. DO be accessible by making it easy to follow you. Make sure you have links to your social media profiles on your website so people can easily follow you. Social media can be full of scammers, and it's tempting to avoid them by making your accounts private and only viewable by people who you approve. However, that's not going to help you sell books or build relationships. The inconvenience of having to request permission to follow you will likely put off potential readers.

7. DON'T send unsolicited Direct Messages. There are services that will automate direct messages for you. They will tell you that it's the equivalent of direct marketing emails. It is not. Most social media users consider unsolicited direct messages to be rude or signs of a scam.

6. DO talk about what interests you and your readers. People on social media are looking for connections with people who share their interests. Talking about those things that interest you will help build those connections with potential readers.

5. DON'T only post about your books. Post about your other interests, themes related to your book and its settings eighty percent of the time and links to your books only twenty percent. Give people something interesting to engage with. If all you post is links to buy your book, followers will quickly tune you out.

4. DO be kind. It costs nothing, and it can do wonders for your brand.

3. DON'T threaten anyone. This seems like it should go without saying, but it's not unheard of for authors to threaten or wish harm upon their critics. Please don't do this.

2. DO stay on brand. Remember, your brand is not just about your logo and aesthetics. Set rules for yourself about what you post and how you respond when people engage with your posts. Stick with those rules.

1. DO have fun. Authors talk a lot about the pressures of consistently posting on social media, but we need connection just as much as our readers do. Lean into the social part of social media. It doesn't have to feel like a chore.

Meet Meredith R. Stoddard

Meredith R. Stoddard is the author of folklore-inspired fiction including the Once & Future Series, a contemporary fantasy series that blends Celtic legends with modern life. She is also a book coach at The Book Grower, the Communications Director of Bookish Road Trip, a community of readers, writers, and travel lovers. She hosts an Instagram Live program called Author Ride Along. She is a contributor to the Launch Pad Countdown series of craft books from Red Penguin Books, and a member of Author Talk Network. Her latest novel, *Thistle & Lion*, will be released on June 8th.

Website: http://meredithstoddard.com/

Leverage the Power of Facebook
Sharvette Mitchell

Facebook has become one of the great equalizers in the world of book publishing recognition. Readers are no longer exposed to just the *New York Times* bestsellers, but every author has the opportunity to connect with readers interested in their writing, stories, and books.

Readers are looking for new books and new authors all the time. They often go to social media for recommendations or to find that next *read*. In addition, readers expect to interact with and follow authors on Facebook. Guess what? That means authors should be on Facebook and active.

This chapter will delve into the world of Facebook through the lens of an author using the platform for marketing their book and personal author brand. Let me say this: Facebook is always evolving and changing. The concepts and thought process for using the platform should remain the same even if a button has moved or the page layout is different.

Let us first start off by talking about how Facebook works. Unbeknownst to many people, Facebook is not just a platform where you play games, see pictures of your friends and their life celebrations, and all of that. Facebook is a humongous marketing and analytical engine. The number one objective of Facebook, as a company, is to build and retain an audience. That objective is shared by traditional media outlets such as radio stations, TV networks, magazines, newspapers, etc.

Why? Because people pay for access to audiences. When companies pay for radio ads, TV commercials, and magazine ads, they are paying for access to that outlet's audience.

The more people that have active Facebook accounts, the more advertising dollars Facebook can command from big companies and big brands. So not only does Facebook want to grow the number of users worldwide, but they also want those users to stay on the app longer. They want users to check their Facebook accounts every day, preferably several times per day. They want to increase the amount of time users spend on Facebook. That is why they're always adding features and adding different things that will entice people to stay on Facebook longer.

As an author, this can be a good thing from a marketing standpoint. Your target readers could be among the millions of people who have accounts on Facebook. As such, Facebook graciously allows us to build our own audiences.

Facebook realizes that most people can become overwhelmed by all the posts, pictures, videos, and content that are shared every single day. Facebook uses what is called an algorithm to figure out what people like and they try to show them more of that content. For example, let's say you have a list of 500 friends. Facebook knows that if you logged into Facebook and saw 500 different posts each day, you would just feel all over the place. So, Facebook tries to determine, based on your behavior, the posts that you like the most, and they show you more of that content.

How does Facebook figure out what people like, and what they want to see?

Well, Facebook is looking for three things on a post: likes, comments, and shares. This is called "engagement." The more engagement a post has, the more it will be seen by more of the audience that is following that page or profile.

When someone likes, comments, or shares a particular piece of content, that triggers Facebook to think, *"Ah ha! They want to see more of that type of content. Let me show them more."* Facebook is looking for engagement to determine what to show you and your followers more often in the newsfeed.

Therefore, an author's goal is to create, share, and post content that gets the most engagement (i.e., likes, comments, & shares). The more eyes on an author's Facebook content, the more potential an author has to garner new readers, customers, media attention, interview requests, and speaking engagements.

First things first, let's make sure your pages and profiles are set up to showcase your author brand! Yes, you need to use both a Facebook Page and a personal profile.

Before we dive in, let's talk about what we mean by brand and author brand. Branding is comprised of two key components; consistency and visibility. Initially, the brand of a company or organization includes the visual elements that make the company or organization consistently recognizable. That includes items logos, fonts, brand colors, photography, packaging, signage, websites, advertisements, flyers, etc.

A brand also goes beyond the visual elements and includes intangible things like the promise of the brand's products or services, along with the story of the brand.

Whether or not you know it, an author has a brand that we refer to as the author brand. The author brand is important because that helps readers recognize you and continue to connect with your books.

Since Facebook incorporates so many visual brand elements, such as pictures and videos, your author brand is important on this platform.

Personal Profile Page

Let's start with the personal profile page because Facebook requires you to have this page first. Most people who are connected with you on your Facebook personal profile page either personally know you, know somebody that's connected to you, or perhaps you went to school, church, or worked with them in the past. There's some connection point that drew them to add you as a "friend" or vice versus. If you already have books out, some of your connections could be readers and customers. The people that are "friends" on your personal page are potential readers OR they could refer readers, media and speaking engagements to YOU.

With this in mind, here are recommendations for promoting your author brand with your personal profile page. These recommendations still apply even if you want to keep your personal page mainly private and for friends. You can always control your privacy options in the privacy settings section.

Intro/Short Bio

At the top of each personal profile page, Facebook allows you to add a one sentence "intro" or "bio." This can be seen by anyone on the web, even if they are not a friend on your personal page. Use this short intro to reference that you are an author, your latest book title and a website address. We want the intro/short bio to point them to your books!

Social Media Links & Website Links

In the "Details section" of your personal profile page, you have the ability to link your other social media sites and multiple website addresses. If you don't see this option on your mobile phone, it will be easier to make the updates from a computer. This is powerful for authors because you can add links for your main website or landing page AND direct links to purchase your book at online bookstores, Amazon, Barnes and Noble, publisher websites, etc. Make sure the privacy settings for this section are marked as "public."

About You Tab

The "Details about you" in the About section is a hidden feature on the personal profile page that some people overlook. However, potential readers and media outlets may look at it.

Similar to the About page on a website, the About you tab allows you to enter your full BIO, book synopsis, contact information, etc. There are no space constraints! Make sure the privacy settings for this section are marked as "public."

Profile Picture

I am sure you have or plan to have a great headshot picture taken to use for the back of your book and other book promotions. I highly recommend that you use the same author headshot (or a picture from the same photoshoot) as your profile picture. Branding is largely about visibility and consistency. We want readers to recognize you and remember you by using this consistent headshot!

Cover Photo

Think of the Facebook cover photo at the top of the personal profile page as a billboard! Create, or have a graphic designer create, a Facebook cover image that promotes your book. You can change this billboard at any time depending on where you are in the book promotion cycle. Keep in mind that this cover image is public so the world can see it!

Pinned or Featured Post

Along the lines of the *billboard* theme of the cover image, Facebook allows you to select a post that can stay at the top of your personal profile. This means that anyone coming to your page will always be able to see this post at the top. The post can be a picture, video or just words. Use the pin post or featured post option to showcase a graphic or video promoting your new book release. Simply create a Facebook post and once you post it, click the three little dots at the top right of the post to select "pin post or feature post." Make sure this post is marked as public!

Facebook Page for Business

Some authors choose to create a Facebook Page for business for their author brand. There are a few benefits of this choice. The Facebook Page gives you paid advertising options that you cannot get with a personal profile alone. The Page has some data and insights on the people that are following your Page and their behavior. There is a section for reviews that readers can use. Lastly, there are additional tools that come with the Page, such as a "preschedule post" option and automated responses for the business Page inbox.

I should also point out a few cons. You will need to get readers and supporters to follow and click LIKE to see your page content. The exposure of your post on a business Page *may* get fewer likes, comments, and shares than content on your personal page. Facebook is a business and have a "pay-to-play" set up. They really want Pages to pay for advertising on the platform.

With all that said, since it is free to set up a business Page, it would not hurt to have one for your author brand! While in your personal profile, click the button "Create New Page" under Pages and Profiles. Follow the instructions from there.

Details Section

Similar to the personal profile, make sure you add a powerful one sentence bio that introduces you as the author or your newest book release. Ensure that your contact information, website links, direct links to purchase your books, and social media links are updated in the Details section. Use the "Details about you" in the About section to enter your full bio, book synopsis, contact information, etc.

Username and Facebook Link

One of the challenges that authors may experience is how to direct people to their business Page. The best way to do this is to ensure that you select and remember the username for your Page. For example, the username for my business Page is "mitchellproductions," and the direct link to my page is www.-Facebook.com/mitchellproductions. The username determines the link to your page. If you have not selected a username, go to Settings & Privacy to claim it. Your name will work fine or match the usernames of your other social media channels, like Twitter, Instagram, and YouTube. This makes it easier for readers to find you and follow you!

Visual Branding

As mentioned in the personal profile page section, update your profile picture and cover image to reflect your author brand. Also, use the "featured post" section to pin posts about your new book release to the top of the page. Try to use two to five consistent brand colors for your graphics and posts.

Now that your pages and profiles are set up and ready to go, let's dig into using Facebook as a content marketing tool for your book and author brand.

Content Marketing is King on Facebook

Content is king. Content is king because content is what you need to share on Facebook so that you can hook your potential readers and customers. It's just like fishing. You must put some bait on the hook. You drop the hook in the water and that attracts the fish. You pull the fishing rod up and there you go; you've got a fish. Our hope is that the content we put out using the features available on Facebook will pull in the readers that connect with our stories, writings, and books. Here are examples of content features on Facebook that you can use to promote your book and author brand, whether on the personal profile or Page for business.

Text Only Facebook Post

One of the most basic and simplest forms of content is a post with just your written words. This does not require any graphics or any special pizazz. In fact, Facebook highlights short text posts so that they get more visibility. If you like Twitter for its simplicity, incorporate that style into your Facebook Page. As an author, I am sure you are never lost for words. Talk about the themes from your book or genre and set the stage for potential readers.

Author tips:

- During the writing process, share how many words you have completed.
- Share the synopsis of your book.
- Share a two or three-line excerpt from your book.
- Share release dates.
- Share book release party details.
- Share reviews from readers.
- Share wins and accomplishments as an author.

Facebook Post with a Photograph or Graphic

Pictures are worth a thousand words, someone once said. This is true on Facebook. Since attention spans may be short at times, a picture or graphic can grab the attention of your followers and readers. This can include selfie pictures or professional pictures from a photoshoot. This can also include "do it yourself" graphics you might make on a site such at Canva.com or you may hire a graphic designer to make graphics for you. Pictures get good engagement on Facebook because followers like, comment, and share pictures.

Author tips:

- Share "behind the scenes" pictures of your writing process.
- Share a selfie when your editing process is completed.
- Share pictures of you opening up your first order of books.
- Share or reshare a reader's picture holding your book.
- Share the book cover graphic.
- Share graphics promoting book release events.
- Share pictures from book signings and events.

Lastly, if your book is available in eBook format or audio format, you should promote that. Many readers are interested in quick availability and easy access on digital devices such as phones and tablets. In conjunction with your graphics and pictures, make sure you post a direct link to where YOUR eBook or audiobook can be purchased and downloaded!

Video Facebook Post

The internet is littered with video marketing stats that all point to the same thing: video is the present and future of marketing. Based on an article by Biteable.com, HubSpot found that 78% of people watch online videos every week, while 54% watch videos every day. In addition, HubSpot found that 72% of customers would rather learn about a product or service by video. This is just a little proof that YOU and your author brand should consider embracing video marketing.

Post pre-recorded videos on your Facebook profile and pages. Just like you would upload a picture or graphic, you can upload a video that is on your computer or phone.

Author tips:

- Have a book trailer video created like a movie trailer and share that on Facebook.
- Record 2 to 5 minute videos showcasing each character in your book.
- After your next author event, record a video recapping the event and share that on Facebook.
- Create videos of you doing short readings from your book and direct viewers to where they can purchase your book.
- Share videos of any interviews.

Facebook Stories

A simple way to dip your toe into the video waters is by using the Facebook Stories feature. Stories are a great way to connect with your audience and share the story of your author brand through less than 25 second videos and or pictures. All content posted to Stories lasts only 24 hours. Stories are full screen, short-form content and Facebook offers all sorts of creative, customizable overlays, which means more ways to be authentic and less pressure to be perfect.

Author tips:

- Post Facebook Stories throughout your writing process to let readers know where you are in the process.
- Post a Facebook Story to leak the book cover design or have readers vote on a cover design (remember, it disappears in 24 hours).

- Post a Facebook Story showing all the places the book can be purchased.
- Post a Facebook Story reading from the book.
- Post a Facebook Story about a reader review.
- Post a Facebook Story visiting book stores.
- Post a Facebook Story of a "day in the life of an author."

Facebook Reels

Reels on Facebook are a short-form, vertical video which can also contain music, audio, GIFS, and other options. You only need a mobile phone with the Facebook app to create reels. Like Facebook Stories, this video content is very short and typically ranges from 8 seconds to 50 seconds, but it does not disappear in 24 hours like Facebook Stories!

Use reels to make videos that entertain your readers and help introduce your books to new audiences. Reels are the best place to grow your audience because Facebook shows your reels to people beyond those that have liked your page or follow you. Include a call to action to tell viewers to follow your page, purchase your books, or comment!

Effects and music can be added to your reel, or you can make simple videos. The reels you create will appear in places like Facebook Feed, the Reels section on Facebook, or your Reels profile.

Author tips:

- Create a reel and introduce yourself.
- Create a reel and tell us about the book.

- Create a reel for each character in the book.
- Create a reel of a "day in the life" of an author.
- Create a reel about your favorite writing tools.
- Create a reel about pre-orders.
- Create a reel about your book tour.
- Create a reel at speaking engagements.

Let me interject this here . . . one of the issues that authors face with video marketing is all about the time it takes to create videos. One of my strategies is to batch record or batch create video content that can be used for standard video posts, Facebook Stories or Facebook Reels. Quarterly, I host a content creation day and record 40+ videos (between 8 seconds and one minute +) that are saved on my phone. I can use these videos for two or three months of marketing.

Here is how I do it:

- Decide a day and time that you can record. Pick a time of day when your energy is high. *Optional:* Schedule any "confidence booster" appointments, such as make-up, hair, nails, etc.
- Brain dump what you can talk about in the short videos. Include things like themes from your book, the synopsis of the book, characters, location setting, tips and guidance from the book, your writing process, current events that tie to your book, holidays that tie to your book, and "day in the life" stuff to help your readers know you a little more. Remember, you only need 8 seconds to a minute for each video.
- Set a goal of how many videos you want to batch record. You could start at ten!

- Pick out multiple tops for wardrobe changes so that it looks like you recorded content on different days. For example, change your top every 3 or 4 videos.
- Pick a location in your home or office that has good lighting or use a ring light.
- Charge up your phone and go.

Facebook Live

We cannot finish up the video content conversation without talking about the power of livestreaming. Facebook Live is a video content feature of Facebook that lets you livestream or broadcast directly to your page, group, profile, or event from your mobile phone or computer. This allows you to connect with your audience in real time as they react, share, and comment during the livestream. A recording of the video is also published to your Page or profile, so it can be watched later as well.

Facebook Live is powerful because it is a Facebook feature that can have high engagement (i.e., likes, comments, and shares) from your audience. In fact, if you go live on the personal profile, Facebook will send notifications to your friends that you are live and that entices them to tune in. Facebook Live is the next best thing to being in person. You can really establish rapport with your audience and readers.

How to use Facebook Live on a mobile device from the Facebook app:

- Navigate to the personal profile or Page where you want to publish your live stream.
- Go to the section where you make a post, and tap the red Live button.

- Add a title/description to your video. You can also tag friends, check in to a location, and add a feeling.
- Tap the GO Live button or Start Live button.
- Tap Finish when you want to end your broadcast.

Author tips:

- Introduce yourself. Share your background and why you started writing.
- Host an online party or pre-order event to encourage pre-sales.
- Take the audience with you on book tours or book launch events.
- Host a book reveal when the first proof copy is in hand.
- Go live when your book is in distribution and people can purchase it online.
- Bring your audience behind the scenes and respond to reader questions.
- Create shared experiences with your readers, followers, and fans with a live reading from your book. Don't forget to direct them to purchase.
- Visit a bookstore that has your book and take the audience along.
- Share reader reviews.
- Share speaking engagement highlights.
- Go behind the scenes of a media feature on your book.

Facebook Events

"Facebook Events" is a feature you can use to draw attention to events related to your book launch. That can include in-person events or virtual events. This tool allows you to create an event notification, share online or offline event details and invite guests. The benefits are that it offers direct notifications & communications with attendees, and it is easy for your audience to share.

Jump start your event marketing

Have a GREAT graphic created for your event. Pictures and graphics get really great exposure on Facebook, AND they are easy to share. Plus, you can add this graphic in the Facebook Event feature as an event cover image. Create a Facebook Event, and share it with your friend list/pages, AND ask your friends to share it, as well. Facebook Events can be created on personal profiles, Pages and in Facebook Groups. Inside the Facebook Event, post highlights about the event each day leading up to the event. Remember: your followers are on Facebook at various times during the day! The highlights should keep this event on their top radar and entice them to participate or attend.

Author tips:

Create Facebook Events for:

- Pre-order sales
- Book launch events
- In person book signings
- Vendor events where you will sell books
- Book tour stops
- Speaking engagements
- Live media appearances
- Networking events
- Book club events

Facebook Groups

One effective way to use Facebook for marketing is to seek out a community of readers or supporters. Facebook Groups may be an option for you. You get to leverage your brand and book and get in front of the audience that somebody else built. When you join Facebook Groups, the group members are people who are not on your friend's list per se. You can connect with readers that you would have no way on earth of getting in front of or getting connected to. Stepping into Facebook Groups and engaging actively inside them can be a great addition to your Facebook marketing. Again, it's a way for you to leverage somebody else's audience.

Always remember to follow group guidelines and rules. Some Facebook Groups don't allow promotional posts selling your book, and some groups allow promotional posts on certain days. When you join a Facebook Group, the group protocol is typically provided in the About section of the group.

How to use Facebook Groups to attract readers:

- Search for groups that have your target market/ideal readers. Closed or private groups work best because the conversations and interactions are typically more authentic and genuine since the group posts are not open to the world such as in public Facebook Groups. You may be able to get in front of prospective readers in various book club groups.
- Search for groups that benefit you personally and build your expertise as an author or writer.
- Engage in conversations on Group posts that showcase your expertise or resourcefulness as an author.

- Share information and tips that relate to your book genre.
- When appropriate, share your website link and how to purchase your book.

Facebook Boosts

We started this chapter off by talking about how Facebook works and its objective to build and retain an audience for the main purpose of advertising. Not only do big brands and big companies have the option to advertise on the platform, but you can as well. Starting at $1, you can help one of your posts get more visibility on the business Page by using the boost feature. Please note . . . there is a more extensive and robust Facebook advertising option in Ads Manager.

Per Facebook.com: *"Boosted posts are ads you create from existing posts on your Facebook Page. Boosting a post can help you get more messages, video views, leads, or calls. You may also reach new people who are likely interested in your page or business but don't currently follow you.*

For example, Jasper's Market posts about its fresh juice menu with a slideshow of all the fruit options. Boosting the post can help Jasper's Market reach new people and get more messages, video views, leads, or calls."

You can grow your Facebook reach organically, which is what the bulk of this chapter is about, or you can light a fire under your current author brand with paid advertisements. Most marketers will tell you that having "do it yourself" marketing on your Facebook Page helps with any paid advertising you plan to do.

Most authors will say that writing their masterpiece is the easy part, but promoting it is the hard part! My hope is that this chapter gives you action items to make your Facebook marketing a little easier.

Top Ten Countdown to Upping Your Facebook Game

10. Add your author headshot picture as your profile picture.

9. Add a great cover photo to promote your next book release.

8. Add a powerful intro and short bio.

7. Add your website address to drive book sales.

6. Add direct links to purchase the eBook version of your book.

5. Add the direct link to purchase the audio version of your book.

4. Post a Facebook Story two to three times per week showing the "behind the scenes" of your book launch.

3. Respond to all comments on your post to boost the engagement and reach.

2. Create a reel about your book synopsis.

1. Jump on Facebook Live and introduce yourself to your audience.

Meet Sharvette Mitchell

Sharvette Mitchell, of Mitchell Productions, works with small businesses to enable them to generate more revenue by focusing on marketing, visibility and branding. She does this with one-on-one consulting, group coaching programs based on her trademarked framework, THE PLATFORM BUILDER®, book collaborations, and conferences.

She is a graduate of Virginia Commonwealth University with a Bachelor of Science in Marketing.

Since 2008, she has hosted an internet talk radio show, The Sharvette Mitchell Radio Show, which airs on six streaming platforms. Sharvette has been seen on CBS 6 and featured in publications such as *Huffington Post* & AARP.

Website: https://mitchell-productions.com

Creating Effective Author Newsletters

Rebecca Rosenberg

An author newsletter is widely considered to be the most important tool for success an author can have in their toolbox, right after their website. Getting yours up, running, and effectively promoting you and your brand is the ultimate goal, but really, it's about connecting on a personal level with readers. Your newsletter appearing in the personal email box of your readers is a privilege to take to heart.

When you think about putting together or improving your newsletter, there are several things to consider. Let's start with what would you like to express about where you are right now, and how does it relate to and benefit your readers? Some authors have a "book club," and review and give away related author's books. Some authors share what they are reading, or what they are feeling about a season. Many offer free short stories in a link. Other authors share their research or travels. What can you offer that reflects your books and your special cache?

As I write this, I am inspired to add pictures and stories about the Champagne region to go with my *Champagne Widows* Series. I led a group of twenty through the Champagne Region of France and focused on the widows who created champagne. I think my readers will certainly find that engaging!

As you gather people for your newsletter, make sure they are the right type of readers for your genre of book. Anyone who signs up for your list on your website is sure to be the right type of reader since they made a conscious decision to do so. You can engage more readers of your genre by engaging in social media where other authors that write books similar to yours are members.

Below is my best advice on how to build an engaged newsletter audience.

First, Do Your Homework

Consider five aspects that make your newsletter stand out in the mailbox.

- *Readability:* Make it easy to scan for the big ideas. Don't make your readers wade through dense copy that they don't have time to read.
- *Storytelling value:* What fascinating tidbit are you offering that they would be interested in hearing and sharing with others? This is helpful in attracting new subscribers to your newsletter.
- *Reader focus:* How does your content interest and benefit your reader? Is it suggesting a new book, a recipe, a vacation spot, or some helpful tip?
- *Clear calls to action:* What one thing would you like them to do in response to this newsletter? Pre-order

your book? Sign up to be on your street team? Post their review? Be clear, and make it easy to do.
- *Attractive, user-friendly design:* Does your design reflect your current books and you as an author?

Sign up for newsletters from your favorite authors, and see what they are providing readers.

- How do they engage their reader?
- What are the benefits they provide to their readers?
- How are these newsletters different or the same as what you want to do?

Check out different email newsletter design and distribution services to understand which works best for you. Many have their own graphic systems that can simplify design. Check out Constant Contact, MailChimp, and MailerLite to decide on one that works well for your needs. The costs will likely be free until you reach one thousand subscribers.

Second, Answer the 5 Ws of the Author Newsletter

Who: Now that you've reviewed other newsletters and thought about who you are as an author, consider how you want to project that image. For example, my bio line is: "Rebecca Rosenberg is a champagne geek, lavender farmer, and award-winning author of historical fiction about glorious women of our past." I like my visceral descriptions as a champagne geek who does not take herself so seriously, a lavender farmer—earthy and unique—and an author who has earned awards for "glorious women's stories."

What one-sentence bio describes you in memorable terms? What images are you presenting to your fan base? Your newsletter should support those aspects of who you are by offering interesting tidbits about each. For example, are you Irish? Southern? Alaskan? BIPOC? Do you have a unique heritage that comes across in your books? Do you play mahjong or play an instrument? How can you use these unique parts of yourself in your newsletter?

To whom are you speaking? What is your demographic audience as it relates to age, interests, and lifestyles? And, are you communicating with them in a way they can relate to? You can get a good picture through your social media by engaging with customers in simple games. An example: I asked in a social media post, "Do you like Sweet or Dry Brut Champagne?" Instantly I could identify who I was talking to and which of my books they might like. I could also tell which readers were not my target readers when they answered, "I don't like champagne." Make up your own target questions and ask those people to join your mailing list! Give readers a reason to sign up for your list: "Join my mailing list for invitations to my upcoming book" or "Join my mailing list for news of my upcoming film series!" (Yeah, I like that one, too.)

What: In a word, content. What would your readers like to hear from you? What will engage them and delight them in your next newsletter?

Content ideas

- *Blog Posts:* Perhaps you've written an interesting post or article that relates to your book. Share a link to your blog or social media page, and ask them to follow.

These blog posts can build interest and credibility for you and your books.
- *Related Memes or Jokes*: There are a wealth of jokes and cartoons available to share that relate to your novel. Check out Cartoon Stock and *Reader's Digest* Jokes for these, as well as many other sites on the internet. You should always be mindful of copyright issues when you are sharing these.
- *Deals*: Everyone wants to know about deals, whether they are discounts or free days, or perhaps your book is featured in an Amazon Prime Deal or even Kindle Unlimited. Be sure to offer the deal and encourage readers to share the word.
- *Background Research*: This is especially interesting if your novel includes some little-known facts, unusual people, events, or customs. Spotlight the most interesting parts and how you gathered the information as well as possibly a link for further information on your blog.
- *Book Birthdays/Anniversaries*: Book birthdays are a great time to highlight your older books to current readers. You can stir up interest by highlighting awards or excerpts of good reviews about older books and offering a free excerpt. Perhaps you can time it with a promotion. Think of how many readers you have gained since that first book. New readers may want to pick up one of your earlier works.
- *Related News:* Is there a news event that relates to your book? Or a travel show or podcast to watch? Link your book to current events or specific interests.
- *Excerpts or Bonus Chapters*: A bonus short story or book excerpt is a wonderful gift to give readers. It can be hosted on your website, or even linked to "Look

Inside" on Amazon, taking them directly to the place they can read the first chapter and buy the book.
- *Giveaways and Contests:* Do you have a Goodreads giveaway to promote? Use that in your newsletter. Or you can offer a giveaway choice of older books or related swag if readers perform a small task. What about a photo contest? Ask readers to post a picture of themselves with your book on their social media feeds. They can tag you to enter a drawing for great swag.
- *Trivia Questions:* Asking questions invites engagement. Maybe you have a trivia quiz relating to your book that readers can answer for a drawing. Or, maybe you pique interest by asking what star should play the different characters in your last book. This puts the ball back in their court, and you can engage them personally. You can post answers to the trivia quiz on your website and provide a link.
- *Present and Review Similar Books to Yours*: If you've loved a book, your readers may too. If you can work with a related author to exchange book reviews and present them in your newsletters, it can enhance both of your readerships. What if you gave the book away as a prize?
- *Invitations to Your Events or Other Bookish Events*: You may have many different kinds of events going on to which you can invite your readership. Invite them to your social media events. Invite them to your live video readings on your Facebook Page. Start a virtual happy hour or morning coffee klatch (Yes, I did just use that term, but hey, I'm a historical fiction writer.) Invite them to in-person events. Invite them to virtual events. Invite them to Throwback Thursday on your

Facebook Page where you prompt engagement with a special story from the past that relates to your book.
- *Awards Your Book Won:* Yes, of course. Show your awards, and explain what they mean.
- *Reviews about Your Book:* Perhaps you share a reader review each month to pique interest and educate readers about how important reviews are and how to write them. Also share editorial reviews from *Writer's Digest, Publisher's Weekly,* other magazines and newspapers, well-known authors, etc.
- *Special Launch Team Newsletters:* Your launch team is special and deserves special treatment. Perhaps you feature their reviews in your newsletter. This not only gets them involved, but acts as a testimonial from your readers. Launch team newsletters deserve special time and consideration to build a strong relationship between you. Consider bi-weekly newsletters to your Launch team to motivate promotional support. These can feature social media graphics they can use, awards or editorial review news, and featured excerpts of their reviews.

What does your newsletter look like? As we touched on earlier, your newsletter should be visual and easy to read. Design it so a busy person can read the highlights at a glance, but someone who wants more can follow links for further information. Think headlines and pictures first. What colors and borders communicate your brand? Should they be bold and splashy, soft and romantic, imaginative and fantastical, or adventuresome and natural? It all depends on the books you write. Have current pictures taken with your book, and use them to personalize your newsletter.

When: How often will you send newsletters? Monthly? Quarterly? Yearly? I know best-selling authors who send newsletters at each of these regular schedules. What can you fit into your schedule? Make a yearly schedule of how and when you will do the newsletter, considering the time commitment to write and produce it.

Where: Where are you getting subscribers to your newsletter? First, start with your family, friends, neighbors, associates, and book events. Next, reach out to your social network through engaging posts that ask people to sign up for your newsletter. Third, try email gathering sites like Book Sweeps, Authors XP, and Voracious Reading. Fourth, separate each group's name so you can sort them and see which readers stick with you or drop out.

Important tip: Organize your list by category, so that you can send appropriate news to each list. I wish I had done this sooner!!! Here are some examples:

- *Local list*, for names you collected locally and would like to invite to a local event
- *Author list*, for reaching out to your peers for reviews or projects
- *Book store list*, for promotions, book signings, readings, and the like
- *Library and PR lists*, to send out press releases of new books or when you land a movie contract

Third, Don't Forget How and Why

How: How are you getting people to sign up for your mailing list? When you ask people to sign up for your list, you can offer a lead magnet to encourage them to sign up. A lead magnet is a marketing term for a free item or service that is given away for the purpose of gathering contact details. Lead magnets can be a free sample, a short story, a book-related article, a fun test, a guide, or anything related to your book.

The second important "how" is: how do you know you are succeeding? Monitor three aspects.

- *Open Rate:* This is what percentage of your emails were opened. The average newsletter open rate is 16%. A good open rate is 20-40% If you had less open your newsletter, examine your subject line. The subject line determines whether your reader opens your newsletter. Your subject line should be brief, have urgency, and benefit the reader. For example: Open now for a free short story! Or, Preorder special on NOVEL NAME today only! Try rating your subject line at https://subjectline.com/.
- *Click-through Rate:* This is the percentage of readers who click on your links within your newsletter. If your links have a high click-through rate, you are motivating the reader to act. If you have a low click-through rate, you need to revise the offer or wording to be more attractive.
- *Unsubscribes*: What percentage of names unsubscribe from your list? It should be under 0.5% of your list that unsubscribe. Analyze where these unsubscribed names came from. They probably did not come from the subscribers who entered their email addresses into your website and consciously decided to join your list. Most likely, these unsubscribes came from a promotional company that gathers names in promotions. This is why it is important to identify or

tag your mailing lists as they are entered into your master mailing list, so you can identify any sources of names that do not work for you.

Why: Why do you have a newsletter? To engage. To entertain. To build a relationship with your readers that grows stronger with time. Yes, and to sell books.

So, yes, please sign up for my newsletter at rebecca-rosenberg.com for champagne cocktails, champagne trivia, champagne quotes, cartoons, and of course invitations to my Champagne Widows Events! And you'll receive a free quiz: What's your Champagne I.Q.?

Top Ten Countdown for Gaining More Newsletter Subscribers with Freebies

Here is a whole page of freebies on your website to attract more newsletter subscribers. Make sure your freebies are targeted to your reader and what they want! Think entertaining, useful, and educational.

10. Seasonal checklists: keeping calm during the holidays, easy packing list for a two-week vacation in a carry-on, etc.

9. An excerpt from your latest book, or bonus original short story of the season.

8. Toasts or jokes to thrill your subscribers.

7. Top ten countdowns: ten libraries you'll want to see, ten top websites, ten things to make a rainy day brighter, etc.

6. Indispensable travel checklist.

5. A trivia game related to your book.

4. Your favorite seasonal recipes or cocktails.

3. Self-love tips to lighten your load.

2. Favorite quotes or anecdotes.

1. Secret strategies sheet: how to make the holiday bright, have the best summer ever, make fall festive, etc.

Meet Rebecca Rosenberg

Rebecca Rosenberg is a champagne geek, lavender farmer, and award-winning author of historical fiction about glorious women of the past including the *Champagne Widows* series, *Gold Digger* series, *The Secret Life of Mrs. London*, and *Lavender Fields of America*.

Website: https://rebecca-rosenberg.com

An Eventful Day
Jade Dee & Wilnona Marie

"We received many applications this year, and after careful consideration, we are inviting you to speak." When this shows up in your email box for the first time, excitement runs through you, then indecision. What happens next? What do you need to know? The idea of speaking at events can be overwhelming for some authors. Proper preparation for the event can help, so let's break down what you'll need.

Type of Event

The variety of events open to authors is as plentiful as genres on a bookshelf because the expertise learned while writing a book is valuable to a multitude of audiences. What comes to mind first when we think of speaking is the writing conference. This is a good place to start since writing is what an author knows the most about. Writing conferences are designed to guide and assist attendees through the process of writing. The primary purpose of writing conferences is to help unlock the potential of students as "writers." Other key benefits of these conferences are networking with other authors and members of the agent and publishing communities.

Not every event will provide speaking opportunities, but each should be considered an opportunity to market your book(s) and your author brand. This is a book on marketing. We want to expand our sphere of influence, and we want to sell books even as we continue to hone our craft.

Other avenues available to us are:

- *Book signings*, typically at a bookstore or library, are opportunities for an author to sit and signs books, answer questions, and sometimes do a brief reading.
- *Book festivals* typically happen on an annual basis. These are events where authors sell their books and interact with the public.
- *Launch parties* are events wherein the author or their public relations (PR) team invites a group of people to celebrate the arrival of an upcoming or just launched book. They can follow the same format of book signings but are more celebratory in nature. Friends, followers, and the press can all be invited.
- *Award ceremonies* for literary prizes often invite recipients to speak.
- *Workshops and webinars* are sessions at which a group of people engages in intensive discussion and activity on a particular subject or project. These are frequently conducted by writing associations, may or may not be for a paid fee, and may be conducted in an online format.
- *Writer retreats*, while not events focused on marketing, offer an opportunity to set regular

responsibilities aside for a few days and focus on the craft of writing.
- *Book clubs* sometimes invite authors to attend in person or virtually to answer members' questions about the book.

How to Get Speaking Opportunities

Being in writing groups both online and in person helps authors find speaking opportunities. Many writing groups hold conferences. Members are often asked to submit speaking proposals before the invitation opens to the general public. This gives writers in the group an inside track. Writing associations tend to have regional writing conferences hosted by a local writers' chapter. Local members are often approached first to speak at writing events. Authors that know the writing conference board can ask what they are looking for that year. It makes it easier to submit. Networking with other authors is a priceless tool for getting a chance to speak. The old saying, "It's not what you know but who you know" applies here. The more people you know who speak at or plan conferences, the higher the probability that they will think of you when looking for speakers.

If you attend an event in which you are not slated to speak, offer to fill in if speakers are a no-show. If you are ready in the wings, you can be a real lifesaver to the coordinator of the event. It also gets you a chance to test out speaking and reach a new audience. When filling in last minute, let the attendees know that you aren't the planned speaker, but that you are excited to share your story. Most crowds will be lenient about any mistakes, so you can use this time to figure out what works.

If you do a great job, other people will invite you to speak at their events.

There are so many ways to get speaking engagements. Look at the website of authors in your genre that you admire. Chances are, they have listed all their media contacts right there. If you are working with a publicist, narrow down the types of speaking engagements that you are interested in and target those. If you are having an extremely hard time getting your foot in the door, host your own conference. That way you can speak on your strongest topic.

Types of Speeches

You may remember the types of speeches from your high school or university days. Let's take a look at how these speech types apply to literary events. And you thought you would never need that intro to communications class!

- *Entertaining speeches* are designed to captivate an audience's attention and regale or amuse them while delivering a clear message. This is the best speaking skill to have in your back pocket. This type of speech can be sprinkled into any arena. Consider inserting jokes or simple, humorous tales into any speech on any occasion.
- *Informative speeches* center around talking about people, events, processes, places, or things. You might use this type when teaching a class at a writer's conference or speaking in a school setting.
- *Demonstrative speeches* demonstrate to your audience how to do something. These are good for workshops, especially when they are intensive one to two-hour

classes. Inviting class participation is helpful for keeping your audience engaged and passing the time. No one wants a two-hour class to feel like three hours.
- *Motivational speeches* are ideal for selling books.
- *Impromptu speeches* are often given at book launches, particularly your own. You may also be called upon to say a few words at fellow authors' parties.
- *Debate speeches* in miniature (less than 30 seconds) are a useful speaking tool when on a panel with other authors and an opposing viewpoint needs to be expressed in a tactful manner.

The forms of speeches are great building blocks. After selecting the type of speech to match the event, decide on a general topic, then break down the general idea into an outline. In the outline include a good introduction. This is where an entertaining story is useful. Jokes are always a gamble, so we suggest sticking to jokes about writing. Inject a little of yourself into the words.

This is also a good time to remind you to have your three-minute or less "elevator speech" that quickly summarizes and engages your listener ready in your back pocket.

Instead of writing out the speech word for word, write the highlights on notecards (or slides) so your speech will have a conversational tone. You can also memorize the speech. However, if you choose to do this, you end up sacrificing an easy, conversational tone that engages those in the room. If you are engaging from your computer, don't hesitate to put notes that will catch your eye and remind you of key points around your screen.

Speaking at an Event

This advice may seem like a no-brainer, but we're going to start off with the obvious. Write down everything about the event, the time, the place, and any technology provided. Then make a list of materials and technology you need that will not be provided. With that in mind, get your presentation ready. Prepare your slides and pack any props in advance for your speech.

When packing for a speaking engagement, don't forget to pack water and mints. If you'll be on stage, wear a few extra swipes of deodorant because stage lights can be hot, and be sure to wear apparel that isn't see-through under stage lights. Become familiar with the technology the venue will be using and make sure your presentation device is compatible. Don't forget to practice your speech to become familiar with your material.

On the day of your speaking engagement, arrive in plenty of time to set up and test technology because tech often has one small surprise problem for every speaker. Any handouts should be ready to distribute. When the moment arrives for you to present, relax and have fun. You have worked hard for this moment.

Bring copies of your books to sell after the speech. Also, be sure to have your business cards or bookmarks for people who don't want to commit to a whole book purchase right away. You never know how that seed will grow. Other printed material at your booth, or on your person, is helpful. After the event, send a thank you email to the group and ask the coordinator/contact person to write an endorsement or testimonial.

Book Signings

Literary festivals and solo book signings are a time to celebrate books. In order to have a good time at a book signing, you must be prepared. In the vein of being prepared, knowing the difference between a solo signing and a festival is important. A solo signing focuses solely on you and your book. A festival has many authors and author-related services. An author usually rents and is assigned a table where they can set up a display and sign books. Panel discussions, book readings, food, and entertainment are often part of the day. They are often outdoor family events.

Ask yourself, when someone glances at your table, what will encourage them to stop and shop? Thinking about what to bring helps you get mentally prepared. For example, you may want to bring "swag," such as bookmarks, coasters, or other merchandise that matches your book cover(s). Don't forget bags for your customers. Authors tend to forget bags, so if you are the only one with bags, you'll attract more potential readers. Also, plan your table display and gather what you will need for that (including a tablecloth). Bring a hand truck because boxes of books are extremely heavy. Take it from people who have had to drag numerous boxes of books around the country. It helps to map out your table position beforehand too, so you can figure out which parking lot is closest to your table.

A Packing List

- Business cards
- A centerpiece or decoration that matches the theme of your book
- Candy (optional)

- An electronic device to take payments
- Cosmetics, antiperspirant, any other toiletries you might need
- A large poster to identify you and your brand and a way to display it
- Books!

Also, plan a practiced, but not overly rehearsed, introduction to your book. This should include an attention-getting opening and the highlights of your book. Consider also what parts of your book match different people's interests.

You'll want to arrive at the event early enough to allow time to set up your table display.

We all dream of our first book signing. However, a vision of a long line of people waiting on a signature is often unrealistic. You can have everything above and still not sell many books. In truth, we barely break even in many cases. If you aren't one of those people that are flooded with fans, don't worry and keep a good attitude. You can still make it worthwhile by taking this time to network with other authors or book services people. Expanding your network is essential to any future success in the writing world.

Host an Event

Hosting an event is a huge undertaking. It is also the one we know the most about. We throw multiple online conferences and workshops a year (an average of 4). We do one award show and one destination retreat. We also plan multiple book tours around the world for us and other writers at least 6 times a year, so we have experience managing events.

Preparation for an event takes organization and personal wherewithal. And, we highly recommend that you work with a lawyer or someone who knows contract law, has previously held events, and can advise you as to your potential personal or corporate responsibility (if you are incorporated) around signing contracts and managing an event. We'll run through a few things to consider before doing an event and how to manage the day of the event.

What should you expect when in the planning phase of a literary event? Feeling overwhelmed at first is normal. We consider five things when deciding if we want to host an event:

- What would be the purpose of the event?
- Who would be involved?
- When would we want to have the event?
- In which state would we want to have the event?
- How much would we expect to spend and on what? How would costs be covered? What might be our return on investment?

If the answers to these questions satisfy us, then we move on to consider the venue. We start with the venue because the venue sets a framework for planning the event itself. Here are the questions we consider about the venue:

- Will it be outside or inside?
- How many people can the space accommodate?
- Will the event be a cocktail party, buffet, or a sit-down meal?
- Will there be multiple events? Will we need multiple venues?
- Is the venue available on the day needed?

- Will the event include a virtual option? If so, will the venue allow heavy-duty cameras? (This is a concern with historic venues.)
- What time will the event begin and end?
- Will the event involve travel?

If you are hosting an online event, then all you need to decide is which platform is the best match for your needs.

After we decide on the venue, we consider the guest list. We begin by asking ourselves who might want to come to this event. Consider how many people will need to attend to make the event financially solvent and whether or not it is realistic to expect that number.

Online conferences can be done in multiple ways, but one simple way is through a Zoom paid account. Zoom conferences can be managed from one link with breakout rooms for speakers. Another way is to have multiple Zoom accounts with each account acting as a different venue under the umbrella of the main conference. Zoom has a webinar option you may want to explore. Other platforms support online events too. A word of caution: before setting up an online event, make sure whatever you choose is user-friendly for the speakers and the attendees.

Once the venue, the purpose, and the demographic for the event are wrapped up neatly with a bow. What's next? Travel. Wherever you hold the event, some people may need to travel to attend. Travel is a problem within a problem because no matter how well you plan for travel there is often a snafu. There could be delays with the speakers, traffic, hotel issues, and the list goes on and on. Even if the event is held locally and your attendees are local, some may want to be closer to the event venue and stay the night in a hotel. As you make travel arrangements, consider:

- What hotels, food, and entertainment are near your venue?
- Will you be providing this information to your attendees?
- Is transportation from the hotel to the events easily accessible? If not, then how will out-of-town attendees arrive? This can be left up to those coming to the event or it can be provided.
- Will VIPs/participants need any accommodations?

After considering these questions, get to work setting up accommodations and transportation as needed. Be mindful of your budget, especially if you are covering the costs of any VIPs.

Here are five things you'll want to remember when the big day arrives:

- No matter how much planning you do be prepared for things to go wrong.
- Staying calm helps to maintain a clear head.
- Make sure your staff/volunteers/contractors are dependable.
- You will be stressed, frazzled, and working at full capacity. That is fine.
- When you have a moment, enjoy what you created.

Hosting your own event is a lot of work, but the rewards can be huge.

Top Ten Countdown to Hosting Successful Events

10. Create a plan.

9. Stay on budget.

8. Stay calm.

7. Take a moment and reflect on how far you have come.

6. Be prepared.

5. Bring water and snacks.

4. Meet new people.

3. Take compliments you receive to heart . . . you worked hard to earn them.

2. Expect, accept, and work to smooth out hiccups.

1. Celebrate your success and enjoy yourself!

Meet Wilnona Marie and Jade Dee

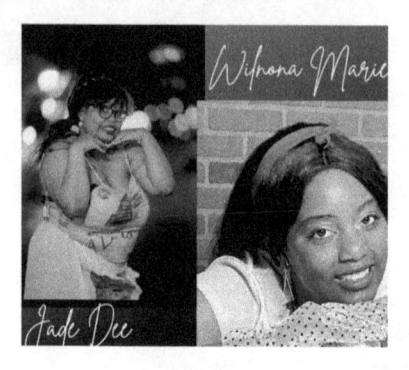

Wilnona Marie and Jade Dee are Advocate Awarded Authors who have contributed writing to eleven books. They are cofounders of The Inspirational Women in Literature Media and Journalism Awards and the 25 *Hottest Indie Authors, Artists, and Advocates* magazine. They starred in the docuseries *Just Writin Life*.

Website: http://www.andwethought.com/

How to Get More Book Reviews
Annie McDonnell

Once the dust settles from the initial excitement of your book release, you will likely find yourself on a quest for book reviews. Book reviews can help drive the sales of your book. You may hear that you need to spend money to make money or you have to be willing to do a lot of giveaways for free to get honest reviews, but there are several wonderful, fun alternatives to spending money and giving away books. It just requires a bit of imagination.

Why Reviews are Important

Being an author is a business. Reviews help build your credibility as an author and encourage new readers to check out your book(s). It is always a plus when others want to post reviews of your writing. Even negative reviews are okay because what one person doesn't enjoy may be what another would. A few negative reviews can even give a book credibility, since ratings that are too high can appear fake.

Book reviews help expand your book's reach among bookstores, bloggers, book clubs, and sales sites. The more reviews, the bigger the chance of your book being noticed.

Book reviews absolutely help sell books, so remind people that they're also helping other readers find you. Chances are they found your book because they read a review written by another reader.

Most importantly, positive book reviews are a wonderful way to say thank you to an author, as they can encourage writers to continue to write in spite of what can be a challenging industry.

How to Get Reader Reviews

The most important thing is that you are asking for reviews consistently in a positive way. Trust me when I say begging for them or complaining that you're not getting them is not going to get you more reviews. That is simply creating white noise that your readers and fans stop listening to and posts they simply no longer read. Negativity gets old fast. I believe the best way is to always be positive, fresh, and fun. Be sure and never suggest that they leave you a five-star review. Always just ask for a fair and honest review.

You must be willing to participate in giveaways. You can find them all over the Internet. Book giveaways often result in reviews, but it is not guaranteed. Goodreads, BookBub, BookTrib, Twitter, blogs, and book festivals are all great places to offer giveaways and build your reader base. Some giveaways capture the email addresses of contestants. This list allows you to email interested readers regarding reviews.

Amazon

Don't forget to ask readers and authors to click "like" on any reviews they enjoy on sales sites. This helps increase your book review average. Even the stars rating alone helps on Amazon. A written review is not necessary. Sometimes readers need to be coached on how to leave reviews. I always suggest to readers who are uncomfortable writing reviews to consider beginning with rating stars alone. I suggest they move up to posting five adjectives once they get more comfortable. Then, a sentence with at least five words. Next, five sentences. I am always amazed by how many of these readers become bloggers or begin an online book club.

There is a whisper I hear quite a bit that Amazon suggests that you shoot for twenty reviews on your release day. It is said that once you hit fifty reviews, Amazon will start using your book in comparison to other books. It is suggested that there are various tiers where authors get more marketing after earning a certain number of reviews. I am not sure if these are rumors or reality, but shooting for more reviews is always the way to go.

Reviews from "Amazon Verified Purchasers" carry more weight in the algorithm. An "Amazon Verified Purchase" review indicates that the author of the review bought the product on Amazon. These reviews are posted directly from the "Orders" page under "How's your item?" in the "Write a product review."

There are guidelines that apply to writing reviews on Amazon, which you can find in their "Community Guidelines." Here are a few to keep in mind:

- To write a review, you need to have spent at least $50 on Amazon in the past 12 months. Promotional discounts don't count toward the $50 minimum spending requirement.
- You are not allowed to create, edit, or post content about your own book. The same goes for services offered by friends, relatives, employers, business associates, or competitors.
- If you ask readers to post a review of your book, keep it neutral. For example, don't try to influence them into leaving a positive rating or review. Don't offer, request, or accept compensation for posting a review. Compensation includes free and discounted products, refunds, and reimbursements. Don't try to manipulate the "Amazon Verified Purchase" badge by offering reviewers special pricing or reimbursements.
- Authors and publishers can continue to give readers free or discounted copies of their books if they don't require a review in exchange or try to influence the review.
- Failure to follow such rules may result in reviews being removed and reviewing privileges being revoked.

Amazon owns Goodreads, which is why they can integrate them with Kindle services, however, they operate independently. For the publishing industry, the main review hub is Goodreads, the Amazon-owned social media site where users can build a profile, share what books they're reading, and leave written reviews as well as star ratings. Unlike Amazon, Goodreads allows readers to leave a review before the book is published. On Goodreads readers can add and rate Kindle books and print books they've purchased on Amazon to give personalized recommendations. There is a Goodreads author program that allows any author with a book in the Amazon database to claim a profile and earn a badge verifying their identity, so be sure to link your Amazon and Goodreads accounts.

How to Get Bookstagrammer Reviews

Bookstagrammers are an unofficial group of Instagram users (who post regularly about books and interact with each other). #Bookstagram can be used to designate a book-related post as part of Bookstagram. Bookstagrammers either write reviews, talk about their review on camera, or host interviews with authors. Some Bookstagrammers take and post amazing photos with books.

The easiest way to follow so many things online, including authors, books, and reviewers, is by following hashtags on Instagram. Search #Bookstagram, #bookstagrammer, and a hashtag followed by your genre to find book reviewers that cover your genre and start following them.

To begin your relationship with a Bookstagrammer, interact with their account, comment, repost, and share stories. Support the Bookstagrammer first. Then I suggest sending an email or a message to the Bookstagrammer asking if they'd like a copy of your book to review it. Email is more likely to get a response, but email addresses are sometimes a challenge to find. It is customary to provide these reviewers with a free copy of your book. Some also request payment. Personally, I'd be leary of that. Paid reviewers cannot post their reviews on Amazon. More importantly, reviews given for free by readers who love your book are more valuable.

How to Use Facebook Groups for Reviews

Facebook book clubs or Groups are a fun place to meet new readers and other authors. These Groups have members who are looking for their next book to read. I have "The Write Review" Facebook Page, which is where I host all of my author interviews. Then I have a Group called "World of the Write Review" where reviews and book sales are celebrated. Each group has its favorite way to promote books and authors. So, you need to look around and find out where you feel most comfortable. A lot of authors run groups, too. I love "Bookish Road Trip," "Blue Sky Chat," and more. There is so much opportunity among these Facebook Pages/Groups.

Look for new book clubs on social media to join using keywords. Join book clubs that share your audience and read your genre. There are some book clubs that will be specific to your genre and others that include it but have a broad focus. If a book club is having a "special event," join if you can. This is a great way to get your name out there.

Once you find the perfect clubs for you to join on Facebook, interact with members, and always compliment their posts. Make sure you become familiar with their readers because they are your target audience. Always promote other authors. You are all a team, and readers notice authors that don't do this. Offer a giveaway or see if they offer "author takeovers." An author takeover is when you post all day about yourself and your book and ask the members questions. You can offer one big giveaway or a giveaway for each post. Keep in mind that one of your posts can be to see if anyone left reviews and ask to see them.

How to Get Reviews in Traditional Media

I suggest trying to get reviewed in publications, journals, magazines, and newspapers. They all have different rules, so be sure to follow them. Local newspapers are perfect for press releases. Publicists are particularly skilled at this. They will charge a fee, but most likely offer a great advantage with their knowledge and connections.

Professional Review Services

There are also amazing sites that you can check out for an opportunity to put your book there for a small fee. Download the resources provided at the end of this book for links to these review services.

- At *BookBrowse* you can post book club questions and more.
- *Bookish First* offers many of the same things to lead you to find reviewers.
- *Library Thing* and *Edelweiss Plus* offer opportunities for authors to get reviews. These two are looked at by librarians when deciding what to order.
- *Fresh Fiction* provides direct links to contact their reviewers. Various programs are offered for authors from eBlasts to Premium Market Services.
- *Online Book Club* offers access to professional reviewers.
- *Pubby* and *Podium* also provide leads to professional reviewers.
- *BookSirens* is a site I enjoy being part of. You can look up reviewers and their "report cards." For example, I'm in the top 5% of reviewers based on reading

volume and women's fiction and the top 10% in reviewing books from small presses. They note that "Annie has posted 148 reviews within one week of a book's release date. This makes Annie a reliable choice for authors who want to create buzz around their book launch." It also says that I mostly review debut novels and more.

- *Libro FM* is a great place to get Audible books. They offer an Affiliate Program with a bookstore of your choice.
- My favorite is *NetGalley*. It is another wonderful opportunity to offer reviewers your book in an eBook format. A member will request your book, and then the publisher approves or denies the request. Often, authors are given "widgets" to hand out to their readers. *NetGalley* is serious about holding its members accountable for leaving reviews by having them share them on *NetGalley* along with the links to any of their reviews posted for your book. Their review percentage is expected to stay above 80%, or they risk no longer receiving the free eBooks. *NetGalley* also sends out a weekly reminder to reviewers. They also reward the members with badges that can be shared on their blog or social media sites.

Librarians and bookstore owners tend to pay close attention to a few well-respected review sites when making their book selections. You should definitely submit your book for review to *Library Journal*, *Kirkus*, and *Publisher's Weekly* for review. However, due to the vast number of book submissions, it can be difficult to secure one of their free slots. Many of these also offer guaranteed paid reviews. These usually carry a hefty price tag and there is no guarantee that the review will be good, but if the review is positive, then it can go a long way to increasing your credibility and the likelihood of finding your book on library and bookstore shelves. If that is important to you, purchasing a review from one of these is something to consider.

Professional Help Securing Reviews

Finding book reviewers can be time-consuming. You can always hire someone to take care of finding reviews for you. There are all sorts of people who offer this: author assistants, virtual author marketers, personal assistants, book marketers, and many others. They often have packages that include reviews. You must find the right person or team to work for you. Many of these professionals will meet with you for a free consultation. You'll have the opportunity to discuss your book, your needs, and your budget with them. They will then give you some recommendations and tell you what they can offer you within your budget. These meetings are gold! Be sure to bring a pen and paper to take notes!

What to Do with Your Reviews

Make sure you know all the places that sell your book and allow book reviews. Ask your street team to post reviews on these sites. Make sure you include Amazon, Goodreads, BookBub, Barnes & Noble, Kobo, Apple Books, and the local Indie book shops, if they allow you to post reviews, on your list. Keep in mind that Amazon is where the Kindle copy of your book is sold. Barnes & Noble is where your Nook copy can be found. You also have the opportunity for Audible reviews on Amazon, or other similar sites if you have an audiobook.

I always love it when I see authors posting some of their reviews as graphics all over the place. Every Sunday, you could post "Sunday Morning Review to enjoy with your coffee"! I remember an author that numbered each review. It was fun helping her grow her review numbers. Post the four-star reviews too! It is not just five-star reviews that help sell your book. Authors should shoot for a 4.22 star average.

Of course, you also want to ask people to post reviews on social media. Great places on social media are Facebook, Twitter, Instagram, TikTok, and YouTube. Let's not forget those online book clubs that you now belong to. I often meander around various online book clubs to see who is reading my book, and then I ask them if they have written their review, explaining that I'd love to see it.

A Few Final Thoughts

Please don't forget that book reviews are not just for new books. I always say, "Books don't expire, they're not like milk." Knowing this, don't forget that you can always ask for reviews. Book reviews are a numbers game. The more books you sell, the more reviews you will have, and the more reviews you have, the more books you sell.

All reviews are good reviews. Don't stress out about negative reviews. They may still bring you a reader or some advice for your writing. Not everyone will enjoy your book, so focus on all the readers that do. Relish those positive reviews. Hold them to your heart and let them give you whatever confidence you need to continue your writing journey.

Top 10 Countdown to Getting More Book Reviews

10. Think of a unique way to ask for reviews at your book launch events.

9. When sending your book to someone, include a postcard with an amazing quote from your book on one side and the following statement on the other: one like #IfYouEnjoyThisBookPleaseLeaveABookReview wherever books are sold and on social media. You can even leave a QR code that links to your Linktree account and the first button to click goes to a place to leave reviews.

8. Begin a newsletter. Include an interview with a book reviewer each month. Encourage your readers to post book reviews where books are sold, as well as Goodreads and BookBub, and on social media. Be clear about how to enter for a free book from another author (or another gift that is not monetary). You can SWAP autographed books with authors for these giveaways.

7. Advertise that you'd love to visit book clubs in person locally or through Zoom if the meeting is long distance. Of course, at the end of these book club meetings, always be sure to ask for a book review and hand out the postcards that are suggested in tip #9.

6. Borrow the platforms of book influencers by pitching them to interview you in their newsletters, blogs, podcasts, etc. If your book is available in other countries, look for opportunities to connect with influencers in those countries as well. During interviews offer to give away a free book, then when you send the book, mention how grateful you'd be for a review.

5. Send letters to authors with similar readerships and offer to give away a book to one of their newsletter subscribers. Getting your name and book out to new audiences will generate new followers and readers, which will result in more book reviews.

4. On your social media pages, you could award a "Reader-of-the-Month." To be entered, you can have various things that readers are supposed to do, including leaving a review on Amazon or Goodreads or both. You can play with this however you want, but people love to be recognized, especially by authors they love.

3. Let your readers get to know you. Once your readers get to know you–your laughter, your kindness, whether you like cats or dogs–they are more likely to leave a review for your book.

2. Amazon has top reviewers, so find the top reviewers of books similar to yours. Ask if they'll review your book. Make sure your letter requesting that they review it is personal to them. Most reviewers on Amazon have their own profile page so you can go there and see if their contact information is available.

1. Consider a paid book tour. There are several options. This guarantees book reviews. A book tour is when you hire another party to send your book (and SWAG, if you have any) to reviewers, bookstagrammers, and bloggers to get reviews posted. This is typically done before your release, with reviews being posted on your release day. They are also popular as a way to celebrate the anniversary of a release.

Meet Annie McDonnell

Annie McDonnell's thoughtful book reviews won a regular spot with *Elle* magazine in 2006. She soon launched her blog, *The Write Review*. After she was declared permanently disabled in 2014, she devoted herself full-time to the literary community and became known as one of its best book reviewers. Annie has written articles and endorsements for authors, conducted author interviews, and consulted with authors on promotions and events. She continues to do so as her health allows. In addition, she administers the *Write Review* and *World of the Write Review* on Facebook. What makes her debut memoir *Annie's Song: Dandelions, Dreams and Dogs* even more remarkable is that much of it was written since Annie was told in January 2020 that she must go into hospice and was given last rites. An advocate for literacy, animal rescue, and those with disabilities, Annie is donating the proceeds from her cross-genre memoir—which hit top spots on Amazon's Hot

New Releases charts in Biographies/Memoirs of People with Disabilities, Poetry/Grief, Death and Bereavement, and Books by Irish Authors, among others—to nonprofits that serve those causes.

Website: https://thewritereview.com/

Book Clubs
Linda Ulleseit

When authors begin marketing their books, they are often overwhelmed by the plethora of possibilities for advertising and promotion—blogs, podcasts, interviews, online groups, book tours, mailing lists, giveaways, events, social media ads, and more. Surveys, though, consistently say that 95% of book sales are based on personal recommendations. Readers discover new authors, then they tell their friends. The friends, in turn, tell their friends and reading groups. That's how word-of-mouth becomes an effective marketing tool.

So how does an author tap into a network of readers to begin that sort of word-of-mouth promotion? One valuable opportunity is the book club. Book clubs consist of people who love to read books. They also love to tell others about the books their club reads. The initial small group of people becomes very powerful when they talk about your book. Book clubs can be an important component of a sales and marketing plan. And they're fun!

Why Book Clubs Work for Authors

Book club members truly enjoy meeting the author of the book they are discussing, and speaking at a book club allows an author to create a personal connection with readers. There's something special for both author and reader about engaging directly over a book discussion. If a book club has had an author attend, either in person or virtually, the members are more likely to tell their book-loving friends about the experience, and about the book. Book club members often become faithful fans and return to purchase subsequent books by the same author.

A book club's candid discussion reveals what worked in the book the group read and if they are interested in a sequel. The informal atmosphere allows authors to talk about their other books, too, or upcoming titles. Group discussion questions, provided by the author, can reveal how well a particular theme, character, or motivation was received by the club. This sort of feedback can guide an author's future writing as well as provide validation for the current book.

Another way book clubs can spread the word about the books they read is by leaving reviews. A visiting author should absolutely ask them to do this on Amazon, Goodreads, BookBub, and whatever other sites are appropriate. With prompting from the author, reluctant reviewers can be encouraged to leave that important review. It's a good time for readers to learn that the review doesn't have to be particularly insightful or lengthy and that a simple statement, with an accompanying star ranking, is all that is needed.

Book clubs are a wonderful way to expand your reach because you only need to convince one book club member to read your book. They will enthuse about your book to the rest of the group and word-of-mouth marketing begins to work its magic.

How to Find Book Clubs

Start your search close to where you live. Ask friends, family, and work colleagues if they belong to a book club. Check with areas where people gather, like libraries, senior or youth centers, universities or colleges, churches, bookstores, and coffee shops. Look for book club postings anywhere you see a community bulletin board or events calendar. Post online on sites like NextDoor or MeetUp that you are looking for book clubs. If your book is regional to an area where you don't live, do the same sort of search in that area.

Many communities have neighborhood newspapers. These are good opportunities to look for book clubs trying to find authors, and also a good place to let book clubs know you are looking for them. If your book is a new release or has won a recent award, or you will be appearing at a local event, the newspaper might write an article about you or publish a news release. This is a great opportunity to say you speak at book clubs!

Online book groups exist on Facebook, Goodreads, LibraryThing, and onlinebookclub.org. It's best to invest some time building relationships in these groups before suggesting your book be read and discussed. Readerscircle.org is a great site for finding book clubs. You can type in a zip code and a list comes up of the closest book clubs. An Internet search can bring up a list of book club guides, some of which are huge. Like any other search, you will have to find one that works for you.

How to Attract Book Clubs

When you start spreading the word that you'd like to speak at book clubs, people sometimes won't respond right away. They will most likely attempt to find you later through your web page. Devote a page on your site to book clubs. Make it easy for them to become excited about inviting you and to find out how to contact you. For security reasons, always use a contact form instead of publishing your email address. Your book club page should include your headshot and speaking experience as well as a statement that you want to speak at book clubs. Post photos and videos of yourself at events. Include your social media links and book links. Most importantly, include a clear call to action —"Book me for your book club!"

Create a discussion guide for your book, and make it downloadable on your website. Choose open-ended questions that provoke dialogue. Ten generic examples for fiction are at the end of this chapter, and many more suggestions are available online. Customize the questions to fit your specific novel or nonfiction book. The discussion guide can be included as back matter in your book as well as on your website.

Another fun idea is to create a book club guide specific to your book. My novel is set in Hawaii, so in the book club guide, I included recipes for snacks and drinks, as well as suggestions for decorations, music, and attire. You might also pair your book with a movie set in the same place. Send the DVD and some popcorn along with your book to the book club.

Approaching a Book Club

Before contacting a book club about visiting them, do your homework. First, make sure they read your genre. Next, find out their method for selecting books. Book clubs often choose readings many months in advance, but some do it as they go. Also, learn a bit about them. Sometimes book clubs have a specific theme or other criteria for choosing books. They also might have members who don't read well, or for whom English is a second language. Find out if they are working professionals, a wine group who reads, homemakers, or writers themselves. Learning about the venue is also important. Planning to speak to an intimate group in a library is very different from presenting in a ballroom or even on Zoom. Remember that you do not have to schedule book clubs around the release date of your book. Plan long-term for the life of your book, which is infinite.

Pitching your book to a book club isn't as scary as pitching it to an agent, but it does need to be thought out. Catch the attention of the would-be reader and share a bit about the book. Include an author bio and point out anything special about your book that might appeal to the group. Is it set near them? Is it somehow related to something they just read? Maybe it is tied to something currently happening in the world. Make your book stand out. You can even promise the club to give them a sneak peek of a new book you're still working on and solicit their feedback.

Time is an important consideration. Ask how long they want you to be there and when. Thirty minutes is long enough to make the effort worthwhile, but an hour might be too long. Sometimes the club wants to discuss the book before the author gets there. Other clubs want the author's input on all those lovely discussion questions you provided. Also, ask if the club wants you to speak about your writing process, your inspiration for characters and themes, or your publishing journey so you can plan time for that.

Send a free copy of your book to the person who makes decisions for the club. Follow up to find out if they liked it and will recommend it to be selected. During this discussion, offer to attend the meeting to discuss your book either in person or virtually. I can't stress enough how much book clubs enjoy talking to the author. They ask insightful questions and have lively discussions. You don't have to attend in order for them to choose your book, but your willingness to speak with them will definitely influence their decision.

Many book club members prefer to get their books from the library, and most libraries will honor patron requests to carry a specific book. Provide your contact with your book's ISBN. Make sure to tell them if your book is available in their library and if it's not, donate a couple of copies. You can also discount books for club members. Have the book club representative collect money from the members and send it to you, and you can order discounted books to be shipped directly to them well in advance of the meeting. Another way is to lower the eBook price to $.99 for one day. Remember that you'll make more sales when happy book club readers tell their friends about your book.

Ask if the book club is open to anyone. If so, offer to help the book club promote that they have chosen your book. Provide them with social-media-friendly graphics, and post about the event on your own social media. You can also send them bookmarks and fliers in advance that they can post or hand out. Make sure every bit of printed matter you send them lists your social media handles and has a line that asks for reviews to be posted on Amazon, Goodreads, BookBub, etc.

If the book club contact you are speaking with doesn't bring it up, ask if there's an honorarium. This may be an uncomfortable ask, but your time is worth it—not to mention your gas spent getting there. Sometimes the club will take you out to lunch or coffee after the meeting, and that works, too!

The Book Club Meeting

Whether you attend the book club meeting virtually or in person, make sure you are well rested. Wear a professional outfit, maybe one that ties into the color of your cover or the theme of your book. If you are appearing virtually, wear a simple solid-color shirt and plan a simple background like a blank wall or a bookcase. Test out your lighting and camera angles in advance. Wherever you present, turn off your phone! Prepare great stories about writing, your book, and the creative process. Bring a smile and enthusiasm!

You should also bring extra copies of your discussion guide. Bring extra books in case no one brought theirs so you can take advantage of this photo opportunity. Also, club members who like your book may want to purchase signed copies as gifts. If you haven't already done so, you can donate an autographed copy of your book to the library or organization that sponsors the book club. Bring a pen to autograph books the members have purchased.

Have a stack of bookmarks to hand out at the meeting, and autographed bookplates for those who didn't bring their books with them. Put a QR code on the bookmarks that takes people to your website where all those other links live. It's also important to bring your newsletter signup list so you can keep in touch with your new fans after you all return home.

It's fun to bring a gift basket to the book club that contains all your swag. You can include the bookmarks and bookplates with a bottle of wine or a batch of cookies. Replicas of your book cover can be printed on edible paper (or ordered from Etsy) and put on top of homemade cookies, or you can prepare a recipe related to the book itself. The basket can also contain a book for a giveaway, either the one the club is reading or another of your titles, and items that tie into the theme of your book—candles, lip gloss, candy, etc. For my book *Under the Almond Trees*, I have a recipe for almond cake as well as some almond-flavored lip gloss.

If the club asks you to read aloud from your book, keep it to five or ten minutes. Choose an action-packed scene if you're reading fiction or a passage that shows your expertise if it's nonfiction. Read loudly and clearly with expression, and make eye contact. This may seem obvious, but it's the first thing you'll forget if you're nervous.

Practice your answers to those discussion questions you've provided. Book club meetings are usually very interactive, so keep your answers short and to the point. Give them a chance to react to what you've said and respond so that a conversation begins.

Don't leave the book club meeting without specifically asking the members for their help with posting reviews on review sites and posting on social media platforms. Share with them that you love doing book clubs and would love a referral to them. Ask if they are in multiple clubs. They won't be able to resist a request from their new favorite author.

Sharing your book with excited readers is fun. They must have enjoyed your book, or they would have canceled your appearance after they read it! They may grill you about sections of the book where they disagreed with or didn't understand character choices, but remember that they are thrilled you took the time to meet with them. Enjoy it!

After the Meeting

Whether the book club you attended was in person or virtual, get each member's permission and take a picture. Send a copy of the picture to the book club contact with a thank you for inviting you. Offer to visit again with your next book or to send them more freebies as appropriate.

That photo or screenshot is promotion gold. Post it on your website's book club page, your blog, and all over your social media. Tag book club members in your posts. Proudly announce everywhere that your book was selected by XYZ Book Club and include the month and year that they read it. Acknowledge their city and their sponsoring organization or where they meet. If any of the book club members tag you on social media, like and comment on the posts.

Hopefully, all the book club members signed up for your newsletter. In your next issue, write about the experience and how much you enjoyed it. Solicit quotes from the book club members about your book and about meeting you. Ask your subscribers to suggest other book clubs for you to approach. Offer them signed copies of your other books, invite them to events, and tell them about any giveaways you are planning. This sort of personal attention turns a book club reader into a fan for life. Finally, remind the book club members to post reviews and follow you on social media.

Investing your time in book clubs returns great rewards. Every author enjoys meeting people who love their book. With a book club, you are creating a deeper personal connection and a lasting memory. Five years, even ten years, later, those readers will say, "Oh, that author has a new book out? I remember when they came to speak at our book club!"

Top Ten Countdown to Crafting Fiction Discussion Questions for Book Clubs

10. Was your attention grabbed right away or did it take you a while to become interested in the people and events in the book?

9. Were you surprised about the ending or did you see it coming?

8. Which character would you most want (or not want) to sit down to dinner with? Why?

7. What did you think when the character did (insert action)? Would you have reacted the same way?

6. The characters can't reach their goals because of (insert pressures here). How does that pressure manifest itself in your life?

5. Describe the relationship between characters. How does their past influence that relationship?

4. How does the main character change by the end of the book?

3. Is there something you would change about the plot?

2. Discuss how the book's title relates to the story.

1. Did the book make you change your mind about an issue covered in the book?

Meet Linda Ulleseit

Linda Ulleseit, from Saratoga, California, earned an MFA in writing from Lindenwood University. She is a member of the Hawaii Writers Guild, Women Writing the West, and Paper Lantern Writers. Linda is the award-winning author of the historical novels *Under the Almond Trees*, *The Aloha Spirit*, and *The River Remembers*. She believes in the unspoken power of women living ordinary lives. Her books are the stories of women in her family who were extraordinary but unsung. She recently retired from teaching elementary school and now enjoys writing full-time as well as cooking, leather-working, reading, gardening, spending time with her family, and walking her dog.

Website: https://ulleseit.com/

How Much Should an Author Give Away?
Renea Winchester

Many writers believe their work is finished with the words, "The End." In reality, the work has just begun. With the launch of each new book baby, authors must find readers. Authors should expect to invest copious time and money getting their books into the hands of readers. However, one must strategically use their business brain, not an author's heart, when exploring ways to reach readers, otherwise, heartache lies ahead. Such is the case with giveaways.

Not long ago, booksellers, book clubs, and libraries invited authors into their world as guests. They lavished authors with adoration, gifts, and a magical form of compensation known as a "speaker's fee." As authors stood at the platform, spoke of their writing process, and read from their work, readers fell in love with the author and the characters. However, somewhere along the way, the universe shifted. Authors were expected to give away their valuable time *and* their precious books.

Friends, I'm here to tell you some good news. Times are changing again. Authors now demand that value be placed on their work. Authors should no longer feel pressured to give-away books for the sake of hosting a giveaway. Giveaways should be strategic and targeted to maximize a return that benefits the author's career.

Recently, I attended a workshop in which participants came away not only excited but empowered to take control of their writing careers. Mandy Ellis is a powerhouse author who serves as a content contributor for blogs, newsletters, and large corporations. In short, she makes her living as a writer. A very good living.

Mandy empowered the group when she said, "Assign value to your content and your work. Do not offer discounts and never present yourself as a cheesy infomercial." She outlined multiple points, with the strongest point being about boundaries. Writers must set boundaries.

I connected with Mandy because her words echoed the message I, and several colleagues, live by: *writers must set their value.*

Your book is a valuable extension of your creative ability. Before you give it away, weigh the positive and negative impact. Give yourself permission to decide what is best for you and your work. Be unique.

When it comes to giveaways, authors are under tremendous pressure to offer book swag including jewelry, free copies, t-shirts, bookmarks, and gift cards, just to name a few ideas currently trending. However, authors who've been in publishing for decades are now asking the question, to what end? Why spend more on swag than they will receive in royalties?

Friends, allow me to give you permission to follow your business model, not a trend. As a writer, you have already given much of yourself. You have placed pen to paper, fingers to screen, or voice to recorder. You have poured your soul into your book baby. It is yours. It is worthy of being read, or you wouldn't have endured the emotional process of creation. Before launching your book baby into the world, have you first determined whether you write for the sake of writing, or are you a professional? Meaning, do you write as a hobby for a tax write-off, or are you trying to make a living as a writer?

How you answer the question charts the path forward with respect to how much you can afford to give away, both financially and emotionally. Before you begin giving away books, you should first take a hard look at how much you can afford. Let's begin with a budget.

Set a Budget

Spending thousands of dollars to market your book baby doesn't mean you will sell more copies. The process of reaching readers is an individual process. What works for Susie Scribe will not work for you. Be unique. In order to be successful, you must find *your* readers for your story, not someone else's.

Setting a budget is the epicenter of an effective marketing plan. An author should invest the time necessary to develop a strategic marketing plan with the goal of increasing book sales and, more importantly, building a community of readers. This goal must be achieved within an affordable budget and begins months before launching a book. Research sales numbers and understand how many copies your genre typically sells within the first six months of release. Be prepared to answer tough questions such as: do I need to invest 7-10 thousand dollars on a publicist who cannot guarantee sales, or is my money better spent reaching readers on a personal level? Plenty of authors invest in a publicist only to sell less than a thousand copies.

My Personal Example

This may come as a shock, but I budgeted a meager two hundred dollars for marketing my debut novel, *Outbound Train*. Where did I spend the money?

- Strategic, local advertising
- Printing press sheets, shipping, and postage
- High-quality stationery
- Non-book-related gifts

Allow me to break this down.

While authors should aim for a national market, one shouldn't overlook the local market which will always ripple outward. Strategic ads in local newspapers and regional magazines are a great way to invest marketing dollars.

Collaborating with a freelance author who will write a feature on you and your book is another excellent idea. It is also free. The freelancer gets paid to write an article; you receive publicity. If you are going to align yourself with anyone in the publishing world, align with a freelancer. Pay them with a gift card, or send flowers. Be kind. You have more books to write and need a freelancer in your corner.

My publisher provided, at no cost, five hundred bookmarks and a high-quality PDF file which I used for promotional materials. However, instead of asking for traditional bookmarks, I requested postcard sizes and used them as mailers. Since my debut novel had a textile theme, I hand-sewed one-hundred fabric bookmarks from recycled cloth which I mailed to the first one hundred readers who either purchased their books direct from me or from the publisher.

Include shipping and postage in your marketing budget. While readers pay shipping when they order direct from you, there are necessary expenses such as envelopes and packing tape, which are often overlooked when budgeting that "free giveaway."

High-quality stationery was a top priority because I handwrote publishing announcements to all the booksellers and book club presidents whom I personally know. Authors simply shouldn't cold call booksellers and ask them to stock their books. Authors should be loyal, supportive customers, too. Each bookseller received a handmade bookmark, a postcard that served as a reminder to order copies of my book, a press kit, and my deep appreciation for their support. Sending book club presidents a complimentary copy of your book will typically yield positive results. Non-book-related gifts include raffle prizes, which I award after an in-person event. Because people attend readings with an obligation to purchase your novel, it is unnecessary to give away your book as a door prize. In fact, I have never given away my own book as a door prize during my career. Instead, I give away something personal, something that builds a connection between me and the readers. Upon entrance to any in-person event, attendees complete a raffle ticket, which includes providing an email address. Why am I asking for an email address? Because I send a newsletter three times a year which allows me to remain in touch with my readers. At the end of my talk, I draw at least three door prizes, which range from local pottery to journals. This "giveaway" is a surprise. It is my gift to readers for attending my talk. They purchase a book. I provide the opportunity to win a prize.

But My Author Friends Give Away Free T-shirts and Totes

I understand the urgency to emulate authors whose "swag bags" seem to entice readers. But before you rush to order a hundred tote bags and shirts to place inside, weigh the cost against the royalty you will receive.

While each publishing contract is unique, author royalties vary between $1.01 per book to $9.00 per book sold, with the average compensation falling around $4.25 per book. Can you fill a swag bag with quality items for that price?

Reflect for a moment. During your travels in the past year, how many people have you encountered wearing a t-shirt with a novel's image emblazoned on it? How many tote bags do you see in the grocery store with a novel's image? Are these gifts accepted and then promptly discarded? Is your money best invested elsewhere? Invest your money wisely for maximum benefit.

Should I Host a Goodreads Giveaway?

The decision to host any giveaway is a personal choice. In 2017, Goodreads reported over 400,000 titles were listed as Goodreads Giveaways.

It is common to see authors who are signed with big houses posting about their publisher's giveaways. The publisher sets the number of books they wish to offer, pays the fee, and the author spreads the word about the event. Goodreads is an incredible tool for book promotion with loyal, dedicated readers.

Once you host an event your "followers" receive notification you've added a giveaway. However, non-followers must search through a sea of other titles to find you. Since you have the choice of offering up to 100 copies, I should mention that a giveaway could negatively impact your book sales if your followers already planned to buy your book. If you offer a hundred copies and only one hundred readers enter, you gain nothing. Set a reasonable limit on the number of free copies.

Reaching new readers should always be the goal.

While large publishers sponsor Goodreads giveaways as part of their marketing plan, self-published and independently published authors bear the financial obligation of hosting their own. It's a given that costs will vary and change, but let's look at the Goodreads Giveaway, as it existed in the spring of 2023, for an example of how to evaluate return on investment. An author must pay Goodreads $119 to $599 for the privilege of hosting a "free giveaway." Authors can offer hard-copy books and/or eBooks. There are two options for a Goodreads Giveaway: Standard and Premium.

Standard Giveaway: $119

When someone enters a giveaway, your book is added to their "Want-To-Read" list. This promotes your book via feeds within your friends and their friends. Those who follow you on Goodreads, and anyone who has already added your book to their Want-to-Read list, receives a notification that you are hosting a giveaway.

Premium Giveaway: $599 per giveaway

Premium Giveaways are designed to give you more opportunities to connect with readers. In addition to all the benefits of the standard package, the premium package also includes:

- Premium placement on Goodreads' Giveaways page with tens of millions of visitors each month, giving your giveaway significantly more visibility and entrants.
- A customizable message sent by Goodreads to entrants who don't win, providing a unique chance to connect with potentially thousands of readers interested in your book.
- About eight weeks after your giveaway ends, winners receive an email from Goodreads to remind them to rate and review your book. This will help other readers discover and decide to read the book and should increase your review numbers.

Let's break down the return on investment for the $599 premium option. Assuming an author earns $4.25 in royalties for each book sold, the premium giveaway must entice over 141 readers into purchasing copies in order to break even. This estimate doesn't include the cost of the books or shipping. In today's market that is a tough sell. With the standard option, an author needs to only entice 28 readers to break even.

While some believe Goodreads Giveaways are an effective way to grow a reader following and increase visibility, it's hard to determine whether a giveaway benefits authors. As with all giveaways, go into the event knowing there are no guarantees you will gain followers or increase sales.

Set a Social Media Boundary

During Covid, social media provided authors and entertainers with a captive audience. We were part of a collective group of "hunker downers," as the late and famed Leslie Jordan referred to us. We were in our homes, desperate for human interaction. Instagram and Facebook Live events provided a necessary outlet that sustained both readers and writers. But now, readers have been set free and aren't as plugged into social media as before. This leaves authors asking, how do I reach the same audience? Enter social media book club groups.

Facebook book clubs provided a breath of fresh air during the pandemic lockdown and still play a vital role in reaching new readers. Book club hosts want to reward loyal members by offering giveaways, and, of course, readers want free books! However, agreeing to join a group giveaway with a hundred other authors for a day of fun is not an effective way to reach readers. Here's why.

Because guest authors aren't assigned a specific time slot, the morning begins with a flurry of posts. As you know, the most recent activity earns the top position on the thread, which means an 8 am post has a strong probability of being forced to the bottom of a busy page before ten o'clock. Authors must then scroll through the group searching for their post and interact with comments in order to maintain a position at the top of the thread. If not, their particular giveaway is lost in a sea of others. Most authors won't compete with a hundred of their professional colleagues only to gain a couple of followers. There is an easier way.

Explain to the moderator that you are happy to contribute if the group is limited to no more than 10-20 authors, or ask the moderator for permission to serve as a guest for a day. In order to include readers in multiple time zones, ask the group moderator for permission to post the winner on the following day.

Individual "author takeovers" provide an entire day of exclusive reader engagement without competition. An author takeover usually features no more than five posts, including photos. Begin with an introduction in which you share facts about yourself and your writing life. The first post also sets the guidelines for your giveaway. Are you giving away a hard copy or an electronic copy of your work? What qualifies the reader for the giveaway? Must they follow your blog, register for your newsletter, or follow you on social media? Allowing eligibility based solely on readers' comments doesn't help you reach the goal of expanding your audience. An effective giveaway will–at minimum–increase social media followers or add subscribers to your newsletter. Otherwise, you, and your work, will be forgotten and your time wasted.

The second author takeover post typically includes a question designed to engage readers on the social media platform, followed by the third post which includes a hook or interesting nugget about the character or storyline. The fourth post engages readers again, and the fifth thanks the hosts and the readers.

Set Realistic Expectations on Reviews

Gifting reviewers and social media influencers with complimentary copies is an excellent way to earn reviews and increase exposure. Book reviewers and influencers live by a professional code of ethics that guarantees your book will receive an honest review and a mention on their social media platform.

Remember, you should deliver review copies several months before the release of your book baby.

Not only do we want to create a buzz about our book, but we also covet readers' opinions. Book reviews drive sales. Some readers understand how desperately authors depend on reviews. We love and appreciate these readers and their kind reviews. We depend on them. Authors should also realize some winners, unfortunately, will never post a review. In fact, winners who don't post a review are part of our "new normal," and are one of the main reasons why authors now limit the number of books they give away. Authors simply can't continue to give away their books without hope of reciprocity.

While it is understood that a social media giveaway comes with an obligation to review, book club group moderators have no control and should not be contacted if the winner doesn't review. It is a personal choice whether you want to nudge the winner after an appropriate time has passed. However, an author shouldn't aggressively pursue reviews.

Set a Limit on the Number of Free Books

I have a darling friend who is a *New York Times* bestselling author. During the release of her third book, I carefully observed how her publisher handled giveaways, particularly ARCs (Advance Review Copies). ARCS are mailed to a group of early readers in exchange for an unbiased review. Reviews post on release day and create book buzz. The publisher expects reviews on Amazon or Goodreads, or both. Failure to review an ARC jeopardizes future complimentary copies.

Release day arrived. I logged into Amazon, paying careful attention to the number of reviews. I found a smattering of positive comments about her work, but also there were 32 "used copies" for sale. How were 32 used copies available when her book was only hours old? Shockingly, people were selling the review copies they'd received for free! It is uncertain whether they also posted a review.

This type of behavior wounds the soul of the writing community and forces authors to restrict how much they give away. If you have an unlimited budget, perhaps you can afford to give away a hundred copies; but as the publishing industry continues to shift, few authors can invest that amount of capital.

There once was a time when authors were eager to contribute free books for every contest under the sun. Word quickly spread throughout the literary community of our willingness to contribute to worthy causes, including giveaways, fundraisers, auctions, and literacy events. Through experience and observation, we now know to limit the number of free books to causes we are passionate about and friends who share our passion. I've found donating my book to the local library builds a readership better than any gimmick. Authors must target their audience and giveaways to achieve maximum results.

Become a Professional Giver

The word "no" is one of the most freeing and liberating words in the English language. If you focus less on the pressure of book giveaways and more on building a relationship with readers, this particular word will result in book sales.

Becoming a guest on podcasts allows you the opportunity to reach a wider audience with the only investment being time.

During an interview, there is one question I always insist on being asked, "What are you reading?"

The question allows me to shift the focus away from me to the books I adore. Words tie us together. Books build communities; they also grow your audience. At a recent literary event in Tennessee, I watched in awe as the presenter stood at the podium with a book held high above his head. It wasn't his book; it was one he loved. When he finished telling the attendees why he loved that particular book, he repeated this process, showing the audience another and another. I shifted my attention to the audience and watched them feverishly writing down the names of his book recommendations. Then after, they lined up to buy copies of his books.

Earlier, I mentioned my newsletter. Sharing recommendations provides readers with honest feedback about books I love. Readers are smart. You have already told them about your book. Give them more reasons to love you by telling them about other books you enjoy reading! In a world full of gimmicks, be authentic.

Here's how this strategy works in the real world. During a book club meeting, someone says, "Renea's newsletter highly recommends *The Book of Marie* by Terry Kay. I think we should consider it for next month's read."

"Who's Renea Winchester?" someone asks.

And then it happens. The magic of free publicity. Your name is dropped during a book club meeting. It costs you nothing, but the rewards ripple eternally, not only for you but for authors you admire and respect. I believe every author reading this segment could easily increase their sales by telling our readers more about the work of others. That is the perfect win-win giveaway.

Set an Emotional Boundary

We've all seen social media postings of other authors giving away every imaginable trinket with the hope of selling their books. If we are honest, we feel we aren't doing enough. We aren't making enough noise. We are failing our book baby. That is not true.

Do not set your worth on something you see on social media. Do not compare your book baby to that of others. Social media provides a snapshot through a window that is no wider than a postage stamp. Beyond the window lies the truth. Your baby is beautiful. Don't be in a hurry to give away the best part of yourself. Your book has value, as do you.

During the excitement of your book's release, remember to consider that some giveaways make sense and others do not. Consider the return on your investment and giveaway strategically.

Top Ten Countdown to Giveaways that Won't Break the Bank

10. Chocolate!

9. Mugs

8. Bookmarks/bookplates

7. Book-themed playlist

6. Book-themed recipes

5. Journals

4. Book recommendations: "What am I reading?"

3. Gift cards

2. Access to free newsletter

1. Chapter One of your novel as a teaser

Meet Renea Winchester

Renea Winchester is an award-winning, internationally-released author. She is the recipient of two prestigious awards: *She Elevates The World* and *Women Who Open Doors*. She is a strong supporter of public libraries and adores meeting readers. After two decades of city living, Renea returned to her beloved Appalachian Mountains where she tends land that's been in her family for three generations. She is the owner of Butterfly Cove Botanicals, a herb farm located in the Appalachian Mountains where she partners with bookstores to offer herb classes. Renea is hard at work on her next novel.

Website: https://blogthefarm.wordpress.com/

Successful Book Promotion Strategies
Mary Helen Sheriff

Once the excitement and bustle of your book launch have quieted and you are typing away on your next book, you may find that your book sales slow down. This is normal, but that doesn't mean you'll be okay with it. Most authors find they have to continue marketing to continue getting sales. However, some authors are reluctant to take time and energy away from their next book to continue marketing their last book.

This is where book promotions come in. Book promotions are when you put concentrated marketing activity around a book for a short period of time while the title is discounted. Because these are quick and low effort, they take little away from your writing time but can get some sales momentum going.

Next random holiday wander around a mall and observe. You'll likely find high foot traffic, many stores offering discounts, and lines at cash registers. Discounting products at strategic times has long been a marketing strategy for high-volume sales and moving inventory in retail. Selling books is no different.

Some Thoughts about Discounting Books

Obviously, Indy authors have sole discretion over the price of their book and the power to set the price and change the price on multiple sales platforms as occasions warrant. Authors working with publishers report different experiences. In some instances, publishers handle all pricing and promotion. Some of these publishers provide notice to authors in advance and encourage them to layer their own promotions on top of the publishers. In other instances, publishers are open to strategizing with authors to determine book pricing and promotions, perhaps sharing the costs. Finally, sometimes authors are entirely responsible for marketing and the publisher happily adjusts the price at the author's request. If you have a publisher, you'll need to check with them about their guidelines around book promotions and pricing.

Some authors are resistant to discounting their books and then paying money to market the discount since profit margins for authors on discounted books are minute. Furthermore, there is an argument to be made against training readers to expect sales, to wait for sales, and subsequently drive the cost of books down. These aren't entirely misguided concerns—you can lose money by haphazardly discounting your book.

However, strategically discounting your book can lead to more book reviews, more word-of-mouth, new opportunities, and more sales of both discounted and full-priced books. You can discount print copies of your book, and some authors find this particularly successful on their own website and for book sales at in-person events.

However, discounting eBooks is a more common strategy and easier to do on a larger scale because eBooks don't have printing or shipping costs, making the profit margin on eBooks bigger and allowing you to offer deeper discounts. For the rest of the chapter, assume this discussion is referring to the discounting of eBooks.

Goals

The most important piece of your sales strategy is determining your goal. Answers to questions like when you'll discount your book, how long you'll do it, how much you'll do it, and where you'll promote it are better answered after you decide why you are discounting your book. Let's explore some reasons for discounting a book.

To sell your newest book at full price. Books sell books. A previous release helps sell your newest release. The strategy here is to discount a backlist book preceding a book launch. Readers buy your discounted book, read it, love it, and then rush to buy your new book at full price. A key step in this strategy is including an ad for your new book at the end of the older discounted book. This strategy works especially well for books in a series, but can also be effective if your discounted book and new book share the same readership.

To hit a bestseller list. The label "bestselling author" has cache. Some bestseller lists have more cache than others.

- The *New York Times* Best Seller list is the most prestigious of these lists. It is important to note that to hit this list your book must be traditionally published and sell a minimum of 5,000 copies in one week. In addition, sales must be made through several bookstores and can't all originate from the same platform (i.e. can't all be your Twitter followers).

Discuss with your publisher whether this is a viable goal for your book.
- The *USA Today* Best Selling Books list was a coveted list open to Indy authors. However, in December 2022 the list went on hiatus and its future, as of this printing, is uncertain.
- The *Publishers Weekly* Bestseller list doesn't include eBooks, which means it isn't a good goal for this strategy.
- The *Wall Street Journal's* Bestselling Books is another list that carries prestige. Be sure to check the categories and make sure your book fits into one.
- Amazon has so many categories that you can likely become an Amazon bestseller through a discounted book strategy. Doing so will result in your book coming up higher in Amazon searches and more organic marketing from Amazon. You can honestly refer to yourself as a bestselling author, but "Amazon bestseller" doesn't carry the same prestige that these other lists carry.

You don't apply to be on any of these bestseller lists. All the bestseller lists above have their own method for gathering sales data. Most use data from BookScan, which captures retail sales of print books at some bookstores, in conjunction with other sales reports provided by major retailers and distributors. None of the lists are entirely transparent about how they get and weigh their data.

To get more visibility. More people reading your book means more people reviewing and talking about your book. At some point, book sales hit a tipping point and the book takes on a life of its own. Discounting your book can help it get there. If this is your goal, then consider pricing your book at 99 cents. Typically, 99 cent books sell twice the number of copies as $1.99 books. This can vary by genre and from year to year, so you should research your genre specifically before deciding on your price point. At this low of a price point, you are unlikely to make much, if any, money.

To make money. The discount price with the highest profitably is on average $3.99. This too is worth researching for your genre and for any market shifts following the printing of this book.

Timing Your Book Promotion

In the last section, we discussed one of the best times to run a book promotion–discounting older books preceding new book launches. You should also consider running a book promotion around holidays. This is especially true for gift-giving holidays and even more true if the holiday can be thematically tied to your book. For example, discounting a romance novel around Valentine's Day can be an excellent strategy. You'll want to plan this promotion ahead of time because several of the opportunities we'll discuss later in the chapter fill quickly and running ads can be more expensive during these times. Non-gift-giving holidays can also be effective if they are thematically related to your book, as readers often get into holiday-related reading moods, like reading scary books near Halloween. The more niche the holiday, the less competition, but completely random holidays aren't likely to tap into any moods. For example, while discounting a book about a war in history might be effective around Memorial Day, discounting a book set in Italy on National Spaghetti Day probably won't gain you extra sales–though it might lead to a fun ad campaign.

Another great time to discount your book is when you can connect it to a current event. This is often easier to do with nonfiction books, but even fiction books can sometimes utilize this strategy. For example, if your novel is set in a country that is suddenly making headlines, you might be smart to run a book promotion highlighting the connections between your book and the news.

Once you determine when you are going to run your book promotion, the next question to ask is for how long. Your goal, one chosen from the suggestions above, will determine the length of your book promotion. If your goal is to make money, then you should not discount your book for more than five days. By abruptly cutting off the discount, you can tap into readers who notice your promotion after it is over but are still enticed enough to buy the book at full price. If your goal is to promote later books in a series, you'll want your book promotion to run for at least three days. Some authors end up finding the discounted price so successful that they keep it forever. If your goal is to hit a bestseller list, discount the book for an entire week. Look up each list's parameters to find out which days their "week" begins and ends.

Where to Promote Your Discounted Book

Just like you can't publish a book and expect to sell many copies without marketing it. You can't merely discount a book and think that will be sufficient to sell books. You'll need to promote the discount. But where?

Your own platform. Post your book promotion on your social media accounts. If you have an author newsletter, send out a notice to your mailing list. These are your warm audiences. They've already been regularly exposed to your brand

and are easy to sell to. However, many may have already bought and read your book. Ask those fans to share the sale and their review on their own platforms. Or suggest they purchase a gift for a friend (do they know they can gift Kindle books?).

Your professional network. Do you have author friends who write in the same genre? Ask them to share your promotion on their platforms and offer to return the favor. Are there opportunities within writing associations to which you belong? Conferences, workshops, and newsletters within these organizations can be a source of new readers and revenue.

Discount newsletters. These are newsletters that regularly send lists of discounted books to their thousands (and sometimes millions) of subscribers. They charge a fee to be included and usually have a limited number of spots, so you'll want to plan and budget for these ahead of time. Prices for inclusion run the gamut. I've paid as little as $5, but some cost several thousand dollars.

Low-cost discount newsletters with strong mailing lists and good track records include Robin Reads, ENT, Bargain Booksy, and Fussy Librarian. These are a good place to start but there are dozens of others, including genre-specific newsletters.

BookBub. The description on its webpage reads, "BookBub is a free service that helps you discover books you'll love through unbeatable deals, handpicked recommendations, and updates from your favorite authors." BookBub is a website that features books and book reviews, similar to Goodreads. Authors can list their books on the site for free. BookBub is most famous, though, for its giant discount newsletters separated by genres. BookBub doesn't sell books. Instead, it provides links to all major eBook distributors (Amazon, Kobo, Barnes and Noble,

Apple Books, etc.). Sales through this then will affect your rankings in these retailers as well.

BookBub offers authors the opportunity to apply for Featured Deals in its newsletters. The menu at the bottom of bookbub.com has a section for authors with a link for submitting a deal. These deals are highly competitive and expensive. The cost of the deal is dependent on the discount you offer and the size of your genre's email list. Many authors balk at the high cost of these deals. However, what they don't realize is the volume of sales that BookBub can generate. For example, when I was lucky enough to get a U.S. Featured Deal in women's fiction, I sold over 4,000 copies of my novel, which meant that even though I only made about 30 cents a book, I still made a profit. It wasn't much of a profit, but I also got over 100 new book reviews on Amazon, was the #12 Kindle book overall, and hit #1 in several categories. Barnes and Noble noticed I was suddenly getting loads of sales too, so they featured my book as the Nook Daily Find, and my novel became the #2 Nook Book for the day. My paperback sales went up too! Last year I did an International Featured Deal. The cost of this was considerably lower. The results were also lower as I pretty much broke even. Still, hundreds of people in other countries read my book. I even hit #2 in literary fiction in Canada. Every author that I have spoken to who has done a Featured Deal with BookBub felt it was worth it. Though, of course, like any marketing initiative, the results are not guaranteed.

Getting a BookBub Featured Deal can be challenging. My novel wasn't chosen until my third attempt. Some people try even longer and are never successful. The application takes only a few minutes to fill out. You are allowed to resubmit every thirty days (or sooner at a lower price point). I recommend doing so.

Your book must meet a few requirements to be selected. There are minimum page requirements for each book category. You'll want to check these for your category. Also, there are rules around a book's discounting history, like how deeply discounted the book is and how long it has been discounted. Featured Deal books must be available at multiple retailers. Amazon-only availability precludes your book's participation. The number and quality of available reviews and your book's cover are also considered. Finally, the selection committee looks for books that have already established some platform, are competitive in their categories, and have professional endorsements from well-known authors, traditional media, major book review journals, etc. Sometimes a book meets all the qualifications but still isn't chosen. This could simply mean that their list is already full, or perhaps they already have a book that sounds similar to yours on the list they are building for that period, or maybe their subscribers aren't currently interested in your subgenre. Trends change; their needs change. If this deal is something you want, then resubmit if you are initially rejected.

Unlike Featured Deals, BookBub Ads can be used to promote any book at any price at any time. Books aren't "selected," so you can launch an ad campaign whenever you want and let it run for as long as you'd like. These ads are placed at the bottom of BookBub newsletters. You are able to target your audience by choosing categories and authors to target. Pricing is done through bidding in an auction format, so you set your maximum bid and whether you want to pay for impressions or clicks. You provide a graphic and copy for your ad (we'll discuss these later in the chapter). While you experiment with different graphics, copy, and target audiences to find out what works best for you, bid low. BookBub provides data that can allow you to compare the variables. Once you find a successful combination, raise your bid.

Facebook and Instagram Ads. Facebook and Instagram ads are another way to promote your book sale. As you probably already know, Meta owns both Facebook and Instagram. You create these ads through the Meta Business Suite. Everything I said about BookBub ads is also true of these ads. However, the ads center of the Meta Business Suite is both more powerful and more complex. This means that these ads can be more successful than BookBub ads, but the learning curve is higher. Some authors choose to boost posts instead of brave the Meta Business Suite. This is much easier, but also less powerful.

Take time to learn how to run a successful Meta Ad Campaign (or hire someone to do it for you) and make sure the materials you use to learn are current. Recent changes to Apple's privacy policy have resulted in forcing Meta to change the way it targets audiences. This means that strategies, targeting, and campaigns that worked before the spring of 2021 are outdated. Many of the people you may hear saying that Facebook ads no longer work haven't adapted to the new environment. David Gaughran's website is a great source for learning more about running Facebook ads.

Both Meta and BookBub require you to supply the graphics for your ad. Two websites that many authors use to design their own graphics are Canva and BookBrush. Graphic design is a skill set. People go to college and get degrees to learn to do this well. Templates on Canva and BookBrush make it possible for nongraphic designers to create attractive and successful ads. Still, not all authors do. If you are going to make your own graphics for ads, spend some time studying graphic design on your own. Involve some of your bookish friends to give you feedback on ads you develop, much the same way you likely involved beta readers and others in your writing and perhaps in cover design. As you test various graphics in your ad campaigns, you may discover that your graphics don't grab people the way you'd like or that you'd like something more original than these two programs allow. Consider hiring a graphic designer to help. The cost of this can vary considerably and can cut into (or even washout) profitability. If you choose to go this route, ask the designer to create graphics you can use over and over or can easily modify yourself for future promotions.

Graphics are only half of the creative piece of an ad. The other half is the copy. Copywriting is a specialized style of writing that is worth learning to do well. Your goal in writing copy is to evoke emotions in potential readers that make them want to buy your book. Headlines are particularly important, as studies show that 80% of people read headlines and only 20% read the rest of the copy. The best headlines focus on the benefit of buying or reading your book, create urgency, and are unique. As for the rest of the copy, storytelling can make for particularly powerful copywriting and that is likely a skill you already have! A rule of thumb, though, is to keep your ad copy short and clear.

Amazon. If 80% of books are sold by Amazon, it makes sense to run ads on the very platform where readers are buying books. Amazon ads work quite differently from the ad platforms we previously discussed. Basically, you'll input keywords (at least 100) related to your book. These can be related to your genre, comparable book titles, similar authors, and your book's themes. Every two weeks you pop in, discontinue the keywords that aren't doing much, add more keywords similar to the keywords that are working, and increase your budget on successful keywords. Amazon recommends running campaigns for four to six weeks. As we go to press, Amazon has three different ad programs: sponsored products, sponsored brands, and lock screen ads. Hiring Amazon's mysterious and ever-evolving algorithm to work for you through an ad campaign can be a fantastic strategy. However, the learning curve for a successful Amazon ad campaign is very steep. Bryan Cohen's website is a good place to start. Be prepared to spend significant time and money mastering this ad platform.

Amazon also offers special promotions for books inside its Kindle Select eBook program. Authors can put an eBook in Kindle Select for 90 days for free. During the 90 days, you cannot sell your eBook anywhere else. EBooks in the Kindle Select program are included automatically in Kindle Unlimited, which works like Netflix. Readers can pay a monthly fee for a subscription to Kindle Unlimited and then can read as much as they like from the Kindle Unlimited library at no additional cost. Authors are paid based on the number of pages read in their book. Books that belong to the Kindle Select program can also take advantage of Free Book Promotions, which means authors can make Kindle Select books free for five of every 90 days. They can also run Kindle Countdown Deals, which allow authors to discount their book for one week of the 90 days. Amazon promotes these books in its Countdown Deals section.

The downside of Kindle Select is that participating authors can't sell their eBook anywhere else for the 90 days they take part in it. This means that they entirely depend on Amazon for eBook sales. It also disqualifies books from some bestseller lists and BookBub Featured Deals. It can hurt sales in countries outside of the United States and the United Kingdom, as

Amazon does not have the same market presence in other countries. Some genres find significantly more success in this program than others. Research your genre's success rate in Kindle Select before participating.

Podcasts, Facebook book groups, and book blogs. While you are running a book promotion, schedule interviews on podcasts, takeovers of Facebook book clubs, and guest posts and interviews on book blogs. Plan ahead so you can support your target platforms ahead of pitching and get on their calendars. Some influencers book months in advance, so this is not a very good last-minute strategy. In a like manner, be sure to check when your podcast episode or guest blog goes live. It's no good to mention that you have a great promotion going on this month if indeed the promotion is either long past or has not yet occurred. Mention your book promotion as part of your interview (post, takeover, etc.).

Stacking Book Promotions

The "rule of seven" is a long-held marketing fundamental. It's the idea that it takes an average of seven exposures to a brand before a customer makes a purchase. Therefore, when you run a book promotion, consider marketing across multiple platforms. You can do this by mix-matching several of the strategies above. It is better to schedule these on different days during your promotion, as Amazon's algorithm rewards consistency over spikes, so spreading out sales over several days is preferred to one crazy day.

A Word about Your Book's Worth

You've worked hard on writing, publishing, and marketing your book. Your book is worth more than 99 cents or even $3.99. I get that. I agree. Your discount price is not the value of your work. It's a strategy to gain visibility and word-of-mouth so that more people will buy your book at full price, talk about your book, review your book, and look forward to your next book. Discounting your book for a few days every quarter can keep the momentum going for your book well after your book's debut.

Paying money to sell books for less profit can feel counterintuitive. However, if you are successful in your book promotion, then the volume you'll sell compensates for the low-profit margin and the cost of promotion. At least that's the goal. There are no guarantees. Some of the book promotion strategies in this chapter take less than five minutes to set up. Some of them are free. Others are more of an investment in time and money. Please do not spend more money promoting your book than you can afford to lose. How much time do you have for book marketing? What's your marketing budget? Consider your answer to these questions in planning your book promotion strategy.

Books live forever. You have time. Experiment. Get your feet wet. Keep records. Measure results. When you find strategies that work, lean into those. Research. Do better. Get help and advice from author friends and marketing professionals when you need it. Sell more books.

Top 10 Countdown to Designing Book Ads

10. Make the graphic the ideal dimensions for where you plan to use it. Different platforms favor different shapes and dimensions. Research this. You may need to create the same graphic in multiple sizes and shapes.

9. Keep it simple. Less is more. Think minimalist and clean. Embrace white space.

8. Use the color palette of your book cover. If you need more colors, then research complementary colors.

7. Use no more than two fonts for your ad. Use the font that is on your book cover and/or a complementary font. You can google suggestions for fonts that pair well together.

6. Look for inspiration. Find book ads you like and mimic them. Take advantage of templates designed within graphic programs and by professionals.

5. Consider your spacing. You want it to be even, aligned, and consistent.

4. Make sure the text is readable.

3. If you are using stock photographs, make sure that you have permission to do so. Some photographs are copyrighted.

2. Proofread your graphic.

1. Make several graphics and test them. Run multiple ads at the same time for a week in which you engage the same audience and use the same copy, but present different graphics. Continue using the graphics that appear to be working and stop running the ads with graphics that aren't attracting readers.

Meet Mary Helen Sheriff

Mary Helen Sheriff serves as an Author Marketing Coach, helping authors save time and money on their journey to sell more books. She's the author of women's fiction *Boop and Eve's Road Trip*, the CEO of Bookish Road Trip, and co-editor of *Launch Pad: The Countdown to Marketing Your Book*. She writes "Journey into Book Marketing," a blog column for Bookish Road Trip, and "The Book Biz," a column in Women's Fiction Writers Association's e-zine *Write ON!* Go to her website to signup for "Nuts and Bolts" for free book marketing tips and ideas every month direct to your inbox.

Website: https://maryhelensheriff.com/marketing

The Magic of Showing Up: Networking, Collaboration, and Community
Katharine Herndon

As the Executive Director of the Richmond, Virginia, based nonprofit, James River Writers (JRW), I'm a wildly passionate proponent of how individual writers can benefit from being part of a larger writing community. My exposure to this concept began with James River Writers' first conference in 2003. At the time, I was a middle school teacher who wrote in her "spare" time. It would never have occurred to me to share with my coworkers that I'd won a local writing contest or been published in a small anthology. Writing was something I did alone, in my attic (okay, on my couch), when I could wedge it in. Then I discovered... community!

If you didn't hear the angelic chorus on that last word, I hope you'll go back and read it with the proper enthusiasm. Community is everything for a writer—both in a feel-good, warm and fuzzy way and in the real-world, show-me-the-money way.

First the warm and fuzzy. Standing in that auditorium all those years ago at my first writing conference, the realization that this entire roomful of people believed in and loved the magic of writing filled me with wonder. I had invested in a whole weekend where I didn't have to explain myself, where no one said, "You write? Oh, I wish I had time for a hobby" or "Maybe you can look at my son's college essay." Without any proof, row after row of people sitting here with me believed I was a writer. On the most basic level, the emotional value of finding the people who get you cannot be overstated. Make it your goal to find these people sooner rather than later and start networking.

With its connotation of stuffy, professional business gatherings, the idea of networking can feel unappealing to introverts and people working in the arts (a Venn diagram with significant overlap). But networking is really a chance to find others who share your passions. Invite me to a "networking event," and I'll secretly roll my eyes and invent reasons to stay home, but invite me to come chat about writing craft or favorite authors, and I'll forget to even ask if you're serving food. By showing up for writers' programs and social hours and being your genuine self, you can find people who like what you write and who like you. Not only will that help you when your spirits lag, but you'll be creating a support system of friends and fans to share your marketing burden.

At that first conference, I had a conversation about favorite authors over lunch with three people. (If you believe in the universe tapping you on the shoulder, you'll like the fact that I'd read one of the authors because my "book-a-day" calendar told me to earlier in the year.) I remember wishing I could hang out with these writers more and prolong the connection we felt. But how was I going to do that? I barely knew them and would probably never see them again. Then I saw them at the next writing program. And the next. Eventually, we formed a critique group and friendships of almost two decades. We still get together to discuss the vagaries of the publishing process, why our characters are behaving badly, and the best (and worst) audiobooks we've listened to recently—and to write! None of us had book sales or marketing checklists on our minds that first day at lunch, but nowadays we'd each willingly buttonhole strangers in bookstores or on the internet to talk up our friends' books. We're a support system and a scrappy street team for each other. Not only did showing up at that first conference launch us into new friendships, but it also planted the seeds for future involvement with James River Writers. Unbeknownst to us, our lunch group held three future conference chairs, a board secretary, a treasurer, a chair, and an executive director. If I'd hidden in the library's gift shop instead of "networking" at lunch, what magical collaborations would I have missed? Make plans now so that you can make the most of potential opportunities.

Start by showing up as much as possible in whatever way is most organic for you. You may have to put in more time and effort in a large organization, but in a smaller group, both the staff and your fellow writers will notice once they've seen you a couple of times. It doesn't matter whether you're attending in-person or online programs, paid events like a conference, or free socials—just start being present. I know at JRW, we're always excited to welcome new people, but we're simultaneously keeping an eye out for our familiar faces, wondering what they're up to, and getting excited about their progress. When opportunities or useful information come up, it's easy to think about active members who might benefit, and we're more likely to pass along those opportunities if we've had recent contact. This year, for instance, a member reached out at the last minute to say she knew our conference speakers were all set, but she'd be happy to help out if anything fell through. Of course, something almost immediately fell through. But there was her name in my inbox. She ended up being on a conference panel on self-publishing, which was helpful to us and to her since she had a relatively new book out.

Offering to help is a thousand times better than demanding that you be given your due. I'm more likely to invite writers to speak at our events who have positively participated in the past, or who say, "I love what your group is doing, and I want to be a part of it!" than those who have no history with us and decided opinions about what they're owed. Don't get me wrong, your writing organization exists to serve and promote writers and bring them together, and it's natural (desirable, even) to be most passionate about your own project. But people will notice if you're only there to promote what you're working on. Plus, you'll miss out on the chance for collaborations and advice if you're doing all the talking. At various nonprofit events, I've learned about programs JRW can be part of and grants I should explore. Once I met a delightful woman who said our organizations should "do something together" and who, because of that meeting, ended up being another one of JRW's board chairs five years later. It's not necessarily intuitive to think about giving as your best path toward getting, but that's the beauty of showing up.

If you want to take showing up and offering to help a step further, explore volunteer opportunities with the organization. Volunteering gives you behind-the-scenes insight, helps you build relationships with staff and other volunteers, and means you get to meet speakers or community contacts you wouldn't have otherwise. JRW volunteers, for example, have met amazing authors like Kwame Alexander, Jacqueline Woodson, Beth Macy, and Melissa Febos as well as benefited from our connections with other arts nonprofits. Several of our moderators have honed their skills on James River Writers' panels and then gone on to moderate for other organizations' events as well, expanding their network and expertise. We also have crossover between JRW volunteers and our local NaNoWriMo (National Novel Writing Month) chapter, between our members and three youth writing nonprofits, and between our members and local libraries. Volunteering with one organization can open the doors to others and introduce you to new circles of influence. Climb the next rung up the volunteer ladder, and you'll find yourself, like my lunch table of conference friends, tapped for board service. Serving on the board of directors for a literary arts nonprofit can look great on your author resume and offers an excellent opportunity to give back to writers coming up behind you.

If you cannot show up as much as you'd like (or don't like to show up as much as you can), becoming a member and/or making donations to an organization can demonstrate your commitment to the community even when you can't be there. Small, regular donations will keep your name popping up on the organization's records and also help sustain a group that is useful to you. Various literary agents at JRW events have noted that membership in a writing organization indicates that you take yourself and your craft development seriously. They like to see this type of membership in the biography section of your query letter, and it can help set you apart if you don't have many writing credits yet. If you can't attend or donate, support your favorite writing organizations and the writers you admire (the big names, sure, but also those just starting out) through social media. Reposting an event with "I love this speaker!" or sharing an author's news with "Congrats on your Book Birthday!" earns heart-eye emojis from your organization and catches the attention of people who are also fans. You want to stay top-of-mind for opportunities and still build genuine connections based on your interests and values.

Don't overlook the built-in opportunities writing organizations offer to get your name and projects out there as well. For instance, James River Writers posts members' success stories (book launches, awards, journal acceptances) on our social media sites and in our newsletters, sells members' books through our Bookshop.org store, and recommends speakers to other organizations. This is not the time to worry about whether or not your accomplishment is good enough or put off sending in your news. You definitely want to take advantage of your group's carefully cultivated mailing lists and social connections. If you've been active in the organization and in supporting fellow writers, they'll often return the favor by enthusiastically sharing your news with their followers. Look for organizations that best fit your writing interests so you can make the most of their contacts (e.g., the Society of Children's Book Writers and Illustrators, Sisters in Crime, or the Association of Writers and Writing Programs). When you're researching the right fit, find out how they support and celebrate their members and what marketing help, if any, you can expect. Some writing organizations will also let you buy advertising space in their newsletters or put your name on a program or panel through sponsorship. If you're considering going that route, be sure to ask how many people you'll reach and think about the timing to maximize the impact. Is there a particular issue that gets a lot of opens, or is there a program you can sponsor at the same time that your new book comes out? Joining several organizations can increase your visibility as long as you have the energy and time. Otherwise, focus on the one that fits you and your needs best.

You may have to give a variety of programs a try before you find out what your writing needs are, and a writing community is great for experimenting and finding collaborators to help you fill the holes. Many members and attendees have stayed involved with James River Writers while starting their own groups to drill down on their interests. One member started a club for writers to support each other as they wrote 540 words every day (an amount recommended by speaker Hank Phillipi Ryan to get to a novel-length manuscript in under six months). Another found inspiration in the burgeoning Richmond poetry community and has been instrumental in bringing poets together for events, critique groups, and even their own anthology. An attendee from out of state enjoyed the conference so much that he eventually started his own version of James River Writers in Georgia. Several have started businesses as editors, coaches, and author assistants. Each of these people found support and like-minded individuals by trying out James River Writers first, figuring out what they wanted, and then adding to their network.

Beyond helping you market to a wider audience, a good writing organization can make you a savvier writer and entrepreneur—and they can do it in less time than if you had to learn everything on your own. One of our former board chairs calls JRW programming her self-directed MFA because she's learned so much, for less money, and on her terms. Even if you're not ready to throw yourself in the deep end of volunteerism, just showing up to learn something can have long-term benefits. We hear from people all the time who get exactly what they need to self-publish, find an editor, or create a critique group from attending a JRW event. Attending educational programming builds your knowledge base, of course, but it also puts you in contact with experts and audience members interested in the same topics. When James River Writers produces The Writing Show (a monthly panel on craft or business) via Zoom, attendees have the opportunity to arrive thirty minutes early and chat with each other and the speakers. So for a panel on editing, an attendee could get a specific question answered during the networking period, hear from a professional editor on the panel, and find someone in the chat who can help with a particular project. Education isn't always disseminated from the stage to the audience, either. By hanging out in the lobby at virtual or in-person programs, you can find fellow writers who have tried the thing you're thinking about trying. Need a cover artist, an expert to format your self-published novel, a social media assistant, or a querying writer to share the monthly cost of a Publishers Weekly subscription? Someone else has already researched that, done that, or is thinking about trying it. Combine your talents and divide the tasks, and the difficulties shrink while the benefits increase.

Here are just a few of the ways JRW members have helped each other out. Two historical fiction authors writing about the same time period found each other through James River Writers and combined resources. They did programs together, sharing expenses and exposing their audiences to each other's work, and also kept each other informed about opportunities like historical book festivals. Two conference attendees met while waiting to pitch their books to agents, practiced on each other in the hallway, and both got agent requests for their manuscripts. Three members started an encouragement group, not for critiquing, but for holding each other accountable for their goals. With fine chocolate and group lunches as rewards, they found themselves hitting more writing and marketing targets than ever before. Another member entered our self-published book contest and got high scores from the judges on everything but his cover. One of the judges reached out, gave him advice on improving the cover, and his book sales skyrocketed. In each case, showing up and sharing led to more opportunities.

I've met people who are concerned that another writer's success means fewer opportunities for everyone else, as if there are only a certain number of books or poems that can be released into the world, and once those slots are full, the other books and poems (and their creators) are out of luck. As if success is pie, and there's only so much to go around. It's definitely an argument against collaboration and writing groups. If it's true, none of the examples in that previous paragraph would have worked. The historical fiction writers would have hoarded their marketing information and lost out on each other's audiences, and the judge wouldn't have helped, because he wouldn't want the contest entrant to become more successful. Besides being a depressing way to live your life, these ideas don't hold up. If you read a story or a poem and fall in love with it, do you find yourself thinking, "That was amazing! I hope I never experience anything else like it as long as I live"? Or do you immediately look for more? More by that author, poet, musician, painter, and more by people who do things like them. "I like Revolutionary War books," you might say, standing in front of two women selling their historical novels. "Give me both!" Success is not, after all, anything like pie. It's more like a pie factory—lots of people involved and plenty to go around.

Before any of this success can happen for you, though, you have to step out of your comfort zone and see what you can bring to the table. You never know what benefits you'll see from the efforts you put out into the world. I'm sure the program attendee who offered to carry our cooler to the car didn't anticipate he'd wind up as our trusted travel coordinator with the emails of fifty-plus high-profile authors in his contact list. I didn't expect to solidify plans with my future critique partner at a writing friend's funeral (though I think she'd approve) or plan to entice a favorite speaker into chairing our conference. Twenty years ago, contemplating attending that first conference, I never imagined I'd wind up as the executive director of a writing group with over five hundred members. But then I showed up. And you can, too.

Top 10 Countdown to Benefiting from Joining a Writing Community

10. Get inspiration & motivation. Be part of a community so that you can benefit from others' enthusiasm and great ideas.

9. Get support. Be part of a community so that you can get (and share) sympathy when things go wrong. You can't all have imposter syndrome at the same time!

8. Make new writing friends. Strangers can give you inspiration or support, but friends give you chocolate and deadlines.

7. Figure out what you need. You showed up, but you still want more. Grab your new friends and build the mini-community you need.

6. Discover new writers & topics. Being part of a writing group means hearing from keynote speakers you're unfamiliar with, getting book recs you wouldn't normally read, and broadening your experiences and reach.

5. Learn from other people's mistakes. Someone figured this out already, and you don't have to waste time reinventing the wheel.

4. Take advantage of educational opportunities. Learn what you want and leave what you don't. There's no homework except the writing. (There's always the writing.)

3. Access a built-in audience. Your writing community already has social media accounts, email lists, and friends. Their audience is now your audience.

2. Build your resume with board service, volunteering opportunities, speaking, and moderating. You can impress people with more than your writing while giving back.

1. Connect, Connect, Connect to other organizations, to editors and agents, to experts, to bookstores, to writers who write what you write, to your literary idols, to staff and volunteers, to people who will buy your books, and more!

Meet Katharine Herndon

As the Executive Director of the Richmond, Virginia, literary nonprofit James River Writers for over a decade, and a volunteer for eight years before that, Katharine Herndon has helped hundreds of writers pursue their goals and dreams. She passionately believes in service to the literary community and has been a judge for the Virginia High School League and the local Scholastic awards, as well as being a panelist for selecting the Visual Arts Center of Richmond's first Writer in Residence, Richmond's first Poet Laureate, and the Virginia Commission for the Arts' Artist Fellowship in Poetry.

Website: https://www.kaherndon.com/

James River Writers: https://jamesriverwriters.org/

Afterword

This brings us to the end of *LAUNCH PAD: The Countdown to Marketing Your Book*. Indeed, it brings us to the end of the series that brought together brilliant authors, editors, coaches, publishers, marketers, and public relations professionals. We came together to share our experience and skills, to uplift the author community, and quite honestly, to jump start others' careers in ways we could have used ourselves. In reading this, and hopefully the other books in the series, I hope you feel an outpouring of positive support from your fellow author–publishing–and marketing communities. Because I believe it is that community that truly makes us successful as authors.

At no other time in modern history has a book's success been so firmly in the hands of the author. We may want to pass some of the responsibility to others, and surely will, but having a basic mastery of the marketing enigma is critical to our work as authors today.

We are extraordinarily lucky that we write in an era where help, and more importantly, community, is literally at our fingertips. In the *Launch Pad* series, we focused on writing, publishing, and marketing as the critical pieces of the author success puzzle. In this book, we honed in on marketing. For many of us, this is the toughest nut to crack, the piece we shy away from, the one we outright avoid, the one that makes us feel most inept, the one we so desperately need to master. But we do not need to do this alone.

I want to profoundly thank *each* of the contributors. From Dan Blank's insightful foreword to Katharine Herndon's closing chapter on showing up, networking, collaboration, and community, I can honestly say that I learned a great deal. I learned new skills and honed others. I deepened my understanding of social media platforms, added detail to the identity of my author brand, and abandoned certain marketing practices.

Perhaps you are like me, one of those authors who believed that as their book launched, Morgan Freeman and Sandra Bullock were going to get their hands on it, call, and Netflix series negotiations would quickly ensue. It hasn't happened for me, *yet*. But I can tell you that Mr. Freeman has held my book. So, I continue to hope and I continue to market, and my life continues to grow and evolve as a result of these efforts. Indeed, this very book series is a result of the connections made through marketing efforts.

This is the main message that I want to impart as we close out this book and series. At this moment, regardless of how well-developed your marketing strategies are, you have no idea where your author career will take you. When I completed my fourth book and first novel, *The Eves*, I believed I was "done." I did the rounds of podcasts, radio shows, and blogs. After over 80 guest appearances, I continue to expand my networking and my community, while I continue to focus on promoting my novel. What was wholly unexpected, however, was that one interview would turn into my being given a spot as the host of my radio show "The Storytellers," which would turn into wider creative collaborations with author Mary Helen Sheriff, my co-lead author on this volume. That collaboration led me to be Director of Membership for Bookish Road Trip and to the idea for my other radio show, "LAUNCH PAD–the radio show and marketing experience that celebrates book releases and the authors that create them."

From that show, it became clear that authors, almost universally, clamor for support in honing their writing craft, understanding the vastly changing world of publishing, and, most certainly, learning how to market their books. Thus, this book series was born. It was a light lift, in all honestly, *because of the networking done as part of marketing*. Emma Dhesi, Scotland-based book coach, came on board to help spearhead book one on writing. Mary agreed to champion this book. And, with that, Stephanie Larkin, CEO of Red Penguin Books agreed to publish the series (the fastest "yes" she has ever given a book proposal) and to head up the publishing book. Because we all also regularly network, we quickly gathered top names in their fields as contributors for each volume. The collaboration between lead authors, collaborators, and publisher made these books a reality in record time . . . 12 months from idea to being able to hold the book series in your hand.

This is the seventh book that I am honored to have with my name on the cover. Apparently, I was not "done." I have no idea what will come next for me and my work. I am glad that after three years *The Eves* still generates royalties every month, some months better than others, some platforms better than others, but each check represents that my goal for *The Eves* is being accomplished . . . *because when our stories are told, everything changes*. I can also look at the caliber of my guests on "The Storytellers" and be in awe that I get to chat with some of the biggest names in Hollywood and also rejoice in chatting with a debut author whose memoir may have captured my attention. Through our "LAUNCH PAD" radio show and the monthly marketing support component, I marvel at the creativity and ingenuity of our guests, expand my marketing prowess, and revel in the collaborations we make with publishers and author organizations. I am not done.

Have a marketing plan. Continue to hone your skills in writing, publishing, and marketing. Continue to write. Be open to your future.

YOU are not done!

Sarasota, Florida

June 2023

Grace Sammon is an author, radio host, entrepreneur, and educator. Recognized in "Who's Who in Education" and "Who's Who in Literature," Grace utilized skills built up over decades to re-invent herself with her award-winning fourth book and debut novel, *The Eves*. She created this Launch Pad Countdown series on writing, publishing, and marketing your book. Grace hosts two radio shows, The Storytellers and LAUNCH PAD. Always committed to creative collaborations, Grace is the founder of Author Talk Network and a member of the Women's Fiction Writers' Association and the Women's National Book Association. She is the Director of Membership for the reader/writer online community "Bookish Road Trip." She currently lives on Florida's west coast with her husband and a small herd of imaginary llamas.

Website: https://gracesammon.net/

Next Steps

We are so excited to join you on your writing journey. For more free resources and downloads, please visit:

https://launchpadcountdown.com/downloads-3/

Enter the password: LaunchPadMarketing.

Be sure to grab your copy of *Launch Pad: The Countdown to Writing Your Book* and *Launch Pad: The Countdown to Publishing Your Book,* available wherever books are sold.